PENNY STOCKS

Beginner's Guide to Learn the Realms of Penny Stocks from A-Z

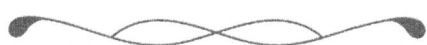

﹥ VON CLYDE ﹤

Table of Contents

Introduction

People across the globe have begun to pay attention to the stock market and learn more about how to invest in that market. If you have ever wanted to invest in the market and are looking for the simplest way to do so, you have come to the right place. You may not have the required funds to invest in regular stocks in the market, so what can you do? You do not have to stop investing in the market simply because you do not have enough money to do so. You can purchase a market share or stock at a minimal amount of $3 or $5, or even $1. You can do this by investing on penny stocks. Penny stocks trading is one of the best ways to do this. If you have watched the movie 'Wolf of Wall Street,' you will have come across the term penny stock. Do you know what penny stocks are and how you can trade in them?

Penny stocks are volatile investment instruments, and it is important that you have the right information before you invest in them. Over the course of this book, you will gather information about what penny stocks are. You will learn more about penny stocks and how you can invest in them. You will also learn how you can make it big since you can make a huge profit when you invest in penny stocks. This book also provides some tips and tricks that will help you invest successfully in penny stocks. It is important that you pay attention to how to invest in stocks, so you do not make any mistakes when you invest. This book also sheds some light on trading in penny stocks and everything else you need to know about penny stocks.

It is okay to make mistakes when you trade in penny stocks, but you cannot make mistakes continuously. This will only make it harder for you to make profits. Make sure that you always learn from your experiences since this is the only way you can make a profit.

Thank you for downloading this. I hope the information in the book helps you make enough profits from penny stocks..

Chapter 1

An Introduction to Penny Stocks

If you have watched the movie, "Wolf of Wall Street," then you must be familiar with penny stocks. In the US, the term penny stock is used to describe low-priced stocks usually between the values of $5 to $10. Penny stocks are also known as microcaps. These stocks are often traded between $ 0.0001 and four dollars per share. Penny stocks are extremely volatile and often show price fluctuations as high as 25 to 100% within short trading times. This essentially means that you can capitalize on these price changes and sell the penny stocks you hold to earn great returns.

Even though they are known as penny stocks, these stocks are seldom worth or priced at a penny. They are known by different names in different countries across the globe. From a legal standpoint, penny stocks are all those securities that are traded within the US at less than $5 per share, and are neither traded nor listed on any national stock exchanges like the NYSE (New York Stock Exchange). These stocks fail to meet the basic trading criteria established by the SEC (Securities and Exchange Commission). In Europe, especially in the UK, penny stocks are often traded for less than £1 per share. These stocks are often transacted over the counter in the US. OTC or over-the-counter is the phrase used to describe any informal trading that occurs beyond the purview of a centralized stock exchange. The OTC bulletin board is operated by the Financial Regulatory Authority (FINRA) within the United States. The OTC bulletin board is not electronic unlike the more popular stock exchanges like the NYSE or NASDAQ. The rules and regulations laid down by FINRA regulate the trading of penny stocks within the United States.

The companies that issue penny stocks usually have lower rates of market capitalization because of low trading prices of their stocks. Since the stocks are extremely volatile, as well as unpredictable, investors tend to be a little careful while investing in them. The success or failure of a business prospect has a direct effect on the price of these stocks. Most of the companies that offer penny stocks usually have no real assets. Often, prospecting firms that deal in activities like procuring oil, mining or anything else along these lines tend to float penny stocks. These kinds of companies don't have a consistent record of their earnings, or even their profitability. Therefore, it is safe to say that trading in penny stocks can be extremely lucrative, but the risks involved are quite high as well.

Manipulation by investors can also lead to volatility in the price movements of the stocks. For instance, investors with a large capital can invest in a large volume of stocks. This will increase the price of the stock in the market thereby leading to volatility in the price of the stock. All those investors who are in the market to make a quick profit tend to fall for these manipulated penny stocks.

The face value of the stock will be elevated to make it seem more appealing to the investors. The current price of the stock will not provide the right information about the business. So, if you invest in this kind of a stock, you must be prepared for any consequences. Since there are such risks with penny stock trading, you should tread carefully. You should always calculate the risks you may incur when you invest in a specific stock. This will help you increase the chances of maximizing your profits, thereby increasing your returns and reducing the chances of losing money. Most companies that have a low market capital do not attract investors since they have zero trading volumes. That said, you should try to use this situation and make sound investments to reap huge returns.

Understand This Before Trading In Penny Stocks

As mentioned earlier, penny stocks are low valued stocks, and these are often traded in the market or over the counter depending on the country you are investing in. The price of these stocks will fluctuate, and you should ensure that you capitalize on this price trend. Before you go ahead and invest in these stocks, you must understand the basics of penny stocks.

Information

Since penny stocks are not traded publicly, the companies issuing these stocks are not listed on any organized and big stock exchanges. This means that there is very limited information that one can obtain about penny stocks. In addition to this, only a few companies issue penny stocks. No law states that companies issuing penny stocks should list themselves in the stock exchange that makes it hard to obtain some credible information about the company. This lack of information increases the risk associated with penny stocks. Like every other investment, you can make a larger profit if you invest in stocks with a higher risk. You can speak to a broker to help you make the right decisions when it comes to investing in penny stocks. Your broker will have more information since he or she will constantly monitor the market. So, it is okay to ask your broker for some help or advice. When you ask the broker for help, and he tells you that a specific stock is not a good investment, you can take his word for it. You should also research about the company and the stock before you invest in it. You should also perform due diligence before you approach your broker.

Liquidity Risk

Before we look at liquidity risk, it is important that you understand what liquidity is. When it comes to penny stocks, you, as a trader, should learn to sell the stocks at the right time and at the price that you want to sell the stocks at. Liquidity defines your ability to sell shares quickly so you can invest in better opportunities.

Liquidity risk is the probability that you cannot sell the stocks or liquidate the holdings at the price that you want to. Your liquidity risk will increase when you invest in penny stocks, especially if the demand for the stock is less than the supply. As mentioned earlier people are not willing to invest in penny stocks because of the risk associated with these stocks. Most investors are risk averse, and will settle for average returns only to lower their risks.

If stocks have low liquidity, it will be difficult for you to find a buyer for that stock. This will mean that you need to reduce the price of the share to a value that will appeal to the investors. Some traders use this to generate profits by manipulating the price of stocks in the market. So, it is important that you understand what it is that you are getting yourself into when you choose to buy a stock. Always consider the liquidity of the stock. You cannot expect to hold onto a penny stock forever. It is always a good idea to buy a penny stock and sell it on the same day. So, make sure that you choose a penny stock that is being traded in the market. Make sure that you collect the right data and analyze it before you invest in penny stocks.

Common Terms

If you want to invest in penny stocks, you should be aware of a few terms that are used regularly in the trade market. If you want to be a part of this market, you will need to understand these terms well. They will give you an idea on how the penny stocks market will operate and will help you understand the patterns you should follow to get started in trading.

Day Trading

Day trading is a common term used in any form of investment, especially penny stock trading. Day trading in penny stocks refers to when a trader buys and sells penny stocks on the same day to make a profit from the differences between the buying and selling prices. The trader will aim to purchase the stock when the market opens or when the prices are low, and will sell the stock when the prices are high. A trader can set buy and sell triggers to help him understand when he should buy or sell the stocks. It is difficult for an amateur to set the limits since they do not have enough experience with trading. Remember that stocks may not follow a predictable pattern, and it is important that you understand the stock and analyze the movements carefully. The prices of some stocks will rise during the first few hours of the day, and will fall during the day. Other stocks may follow the opposite pattern. Penny stocks are traded differently in different countries, and you should understand the differences before you begin trading in different countries.

Due Diligence

Before you decide on which stock you should buy, it is important that you perform your due diligence (DD). This is a term that is used often in investing, especially in penny stock trading. It is important that you assess the company and the stock before you buy the stock. You should ensure that you obtain this information from reliable sources, so you do not have to risk your funds. Assess the data you collect and analyze it to verify if a stock you want to invest in is good or bad. You can make these decisions based on the price fluctuations. Ensure that you study the data carefully and assess if the stock will give you good returns. You will find information about the stock on the Internet, and you can use that information to conduct the analysis. Do not assume that the stock will be good because people have bought it. People tend to buy a stock too much using some information shared by the management.

Stop Loss Percentage

You will also hear the term stop loss percentage frequently when you trade. This percentage is a value that you set to determine to what extent you can take a loss. If you set the percentage to 10%, and the value of the stock that you invested in begins to fall by 10%, you should let go of that stock so you can maintain your capital and accept the loss. This is an extremely important percentage that you should bear in mind when it comes to trading in the stock market, and this is especially true for penny stock traders. Many traders worry that they will incur a loss if they sell a stock without waiting for the price to increase. This is a wrong way to approach the situation. If you wait for the price to increase, you may lose out on an opportunity to make a profit. You may also risk getting your capital stuck in that stock alone. You should instead choose to assume a position from the same place or invest in a better stock. If you use this method, you can ensure that your capital is not locked in a bad investment. Consider the following example: if you buy 100 stocks from a company at $1 each, you will have invested $100 of your capital in that stock. You hope that the price of the stock will increase to $1.05 by the end of the day. You should place a stop loss percentage of 10$ on that stock if the price drops to lower than what you expected. So, you should set your stop loss amount at $0.90. If the price of the stock falls to that number, you know that you should let go of the stock.

Swinging

Swinging is a term that refers to when you exit the market at your stop loss mark and take a fresh position right there. The objective behind swinging is to capitalize on the volatility of the stock and cover any losses that you may make. The belief is that the price of a stock will increase steadily if it hits a low. So, when the stock reaches the lowest price, you should know that it would rise again. A trader will always prefer to place a stop loss at this point before he or she incurs a loss. You should ensure that you choose the ten percent cover when you set the stop loss. Never underestimate the value of the stop loss method, and try to put that into practice.

Ask

The "ask" is the practical share price that is acceptable at a specific moment when you are trading in shares. This is the price that you, as a trader, will ask for a share. You believe that the ask price of the stock will be the best value for that stock. The ask price is dependent on the analysis that you perform about the stock. You can judge the price of a stock only when you study the market and the stocks for a while. People set very low ask values and you may wonder if you are setting the wrong ask value if you place a lower amount. If you do perform the right research, you will learn that the price of the stock is falling and that you will gain from the trade. You should also study the market to decide on what the ideal ask price is for different stocks.

Profit Percentage Gain

You as a trader must set a profit percentage gain. This percentage will give the broker an idea of where you have pegged the profits. As a trader, you can make a profit if you stick to the profit percentage gain. You can calculate this percentage based on when you buy or sell the stocks and at what price. Every trader has some expectations regarding their investments, and they will decide the stocks they should invest in based on their profit percentage gain.

Bid

The bid refers to price at which the stocks are sold in the market.

Volume

The volume of the stock is the number of shares that you can trade at any point in the market. The volume of stocks in the market will constantly change since the ask price of one individual will match the bid price of the stock. This type of matching will occur at multiple points throughout the day, and the volume will never remain stable. It will fluctuate throughout the day and there is no tool or software that will help you assess how the volumes will fluctuate. A penny stock will also have volume fluctuations throughout the day, and the volumes will not stabilize at any point until the price of the stock remains constant because of excess buyers or sellers.

Broker

A broker is someone who will help you trade your stocks. If you are not a member of the stock exchange, you cannot trade in the stock market. For this, you must take the help of your broker. A broker is part of a company that is a member of the stock exchange, and it is for this reason that he or she can help you with buying and selling stocks. The broker can also advise you on which stocks you should invest in, and will tell you whether or not you are making the right decisions. The final decision, however, is yours. You can trust the broker fully, or perform some analysis to assess whether the stock is indeed good to invest in. You can choose between a full-time and a part-time broker. A full-time broker is someone who will constantly work on your profile, and will trade in the market to ensure that you make a profit. This broker will look at the trends of the market and alert you if there is a good deal that they come across. A part time broker is someone who will only buy and sell your stocks. He will not give you advice or spend time to help to maximize your profits. The former will charge you more since he spends all his time on investing for you. This book lists different types of brokers you can consider or approach. Make sure that you always look for a broker who is reliable and trustworthy. Ask people you know about a broker they will recommend. You can also read the testimonials to see which broker you should approach. These testimonials are proof of whom you can and cannot trust.

Commission

You must pay the broker some commission for the services that he or she provides. This broker will help you buy and sell stocks, and may also give you some suggestions. For this, they will charge you a commission. The amount that is deducted from your profit does not go only to the broker. Some of the commission will go to the company as well. The commission charged will vary from one company to another. You should pick the company that charges the lowest rate. If you do not want to compromise on quality and are willing to spend more, you can choose a good broker. Having said that, you must assess the company to see if it is good, and whether the brokers in that company are good at what they do. You can also request the company to assign you to a broker who has a good reputation.

Limit order

The limit order refers to the price at which you want to sell your stock. This point is where your stocks will be sold. You must instruct your broker and ensure that he is aware that he should never sell a stock at a price lower than the limit order. You will have calculated your profit margin based on the limit order, and you must ensure that you stick to that percentage gain. Numerous software and applications can help you set this price yourself, so that the stock you own is sold the minute it reaches that price. You do not have to track the price constantly.

Portfolio

The portfolio you maintain is your investment sheet. This will hold the information about all the investments you make, and will include details about the stocks you hold, the ones you sold, stock value, number, the price at which the stock was bought, profit made, unrealized profits and more. These details are important to maintain, and you must understand the information. Using this investment sheet, you can also see the trend that you maintained when it comes to buying and selling stocks. You should look at your portfolio at the end of the day to assess your performance and verify if you have traded the right stocks or not. If you identify any errors in the portfolio, you should correct them immediately.

Stock Split

The stock split refers to how the company splits the stock into two or more stocks to increase the number of stocks available in the market. The company does this when the stocks are bought quickly, and people are not willing to let go of the shares they hold. The company needs to pump in more shares into the market to increase the market capture. It is a good thing if this happens, especially if you hold penny stocks. When you hear the announcement, you will know how many bonus shares are available. This will help you make a greater profit.

Bullish Reversal

A bullish reversal refers to the change in the price of the stock. When the price of a stock constantly moves upward, the stock is said to follow a bullish trend. This will only happen if the lowest of the low price on the previous day and the current price of the stock is higher than the price of the stock at the close of the market on the previous day. So, the price of the stock will move upward, and the trend will help you realize if you are investing to make a profit or a loss. This trend will occur only when there are more buyers than sellers in the market, and the demand is greater than the supply. You should capitalize on this situation and sell the stocks, so you make a profit. The price of the stock will continue to rise which will make it easier for you to dispose the stocks you have. You will, however, need to make these decisions quickly. It is hard to predict if the price of the stock will continue to rise or remain at the same rate. An inexperienced hand will find it hard to judge the situation and make the right decision. They cannot determine how the price of the stock will move.

Bearish Reversal

The bearish reversal is completely the opposite of bullish reversal. This situation occurs when the price of the stock today is lower than the price at close yesterday. This is a downward trend in the price of the stock. This will appear when numerous people sell their stocks together. This trend will make you lose money on some bad stocks. When the stock follows this pattern, it is difficult to understand the trend. The stock price can either move upwards or downwards depending on the market. In this case, it is best to wait for the prices to change before you choose to sell or keep the stock. So, wait for the price to stabilize before you make your decision. If you think the stock will continue to follow this trend, you should sell the stock immediately.

The Theory of Demand and Supply

It is important to remember that it is the theory of demand and supply that affects the price of any stock in the market, including penny stocks. If a stock is in demand and the supply of that stock is low, then the price will increase. This will happen since there are more people who want to buy the stock and there are very few stocks in the market. In this instance, you should check the number of sellers and the number of shares against each seller in the market. This will help you understand if the price will increase or if is best to adopt the bearish bar reversal before you invest in that stock. The price of the stock will decrease when there are too many sellers and too many stocks in the market, but very little demand. The price of such a stock will drastically decrease. If there are too many stocks in the market, and very few buyers the price will drop. Ensure that you enter the market by investing in the right stock.

If you observe the trend of different stocks in the market, you will know when the price of a stock dips. You should invest in the stock during the dip since it will help you average the price out. This is a great way to help you reduce the price of the share. For example, if you bought 100 shares for $2 each, you paid $200. If the price drops to $1, you should purchase another 100 shares at that rate. This will change the overall price of each of your 200 shares to $1.5. When you sell these shares, you will make a profit. Let us look at how the process of trading in penny stocks looks like:

1. Perform due diligence to assess which stocks you should invest in. You must perform research and identify the list of stocks that you want to consider trading in for that day.

2. Using your judgment, assess the reaction of the market and choose one of the stocks.

3. Purchase the stocks.

4. When you think that you will make a profit, sell the stocks.

Continue this process until you let go of all the stocks that you purchase. We will look at this process in detail over the course of the book.:

Chapter 2

Getting Started with Penny Stock Trading

If you are an amateur in Penny stocks trading, it is prudent that you begin with paper trading. In this type of trading you will use fake money to trade instead of your hard-earned money. So, take some time to learn what penny stock trading is all about before you test your skills in the market. You should ensure that you record all your results. This will give you enough confidence to help you to trade in the actual market. When you are sure about your skills, you can then setup an online broker account to begin trading in Penny stocks. Before you start reading in Penny stocks, you need to invest in some tools. This chapter sheds some light on the different tools that you will need especially if you want to start trading on Penny stocks online.

Reliable Computer

It is important to invest in a good computer to ensure that you do not have any trouble with trading online. If you wish to trade online, you will need to ensure that you do not have any trouble because of computer failure or the inability of your computer to process any orders. You must ensure that you get the right computer to serve your purpose. Make sure you have a dedicated computer table and computer for online trading alone. Never allow any other user to access this computer and ensure you are the only person who can work on this computer. You need to ensure that nobody has access to the data on this computer. Remember to take this very seriously if you want to make it big in the stock market. If you have a casual attitude about reading, you will not make it big. If you decide that you want to purchase a laptop, make sure that it is not constantly moved around. Choose a spot in your house or at office where you can place your laptop and make sure that you reach the laptop on time every day before the market opens and conductor early research.

Reliable Internet Connection

Since you are trading online it is important that you have very good Internet connection. As mentioned earlier, the prices of stocks rise very quickly which means that you must be on the lookout for any changes in the price and make a suitable decision at the right time. If you have an unreliable Internet connection, you will lose the chance to the buy or sell stocks at the right time. The risk will increase if you want to be a part of the day trading session. The prices of the stock will vary during the day in a matter of seconds, and it is important that you grasp the opportunity to buy or sell the stock at the lowest or highest prices respectively. If you have issues with the Internet, then you cannot use price fluctuation and will lose out and making a large profit. So, it is important that you get the fastest Internet connection, so you do not lose out on making money.

Brokering Company

Now, you will need to choose a broking firm. Before you pick a brokering company, you must assess whether the company offers the best commission rate or not. Ensure that you choose the company that is right for you. You can also ask someone you know to suggest a brokering company they believe is the best. Alternatively, you can conduct research on the Internet to identify the best one. When you decide on the company, visit the office and fill the necessary forms. You may need to carry a few documents to register yourself at the firm.

Special Broker

Once you choose the firm and also open your account, you should identify the right broker to help you with investing in the right stocks. There are many penny stocks specialists who will help you understand what a penny stock is and how it functions. You must speak to the firm and ask them to suggest the best broker to help you with investing in the market. Remember, you must develop a good rapport with your broker if you want to make it big. There must be no differences between your views about the market or the profit you can make. It is for this reason that you must always ensure that you and the broker are on the same page.

Trading Software with Real Time Data

Once you have identified the broker, the firm and established good Internet connectivity, you should identify the right software or application that you can use to assess Penny stocks. It is important that you always use real time data when you trade in Penny stocks. This will ensure that you do not make decisions based on outdated information that can cost you a lot of money. You can download the software or tools from the Internet. You can also download some applications on your phone from the app store. It is, however, easier to speak to the brokering company to help you identify the right software to use. It is also a good idea to choose the same application that your broker uses. If you do not want to depend on the broker, you can look for different software on Internet. These tools will help you buy and sell stocks by yourself. You only need to login and place a bid on a stock or sell it. This way you do not waste time in speaking to your broker before you buy or sell stock. Before you do this, it is important that you understand how to choose a penny stock to buy or sell, so you reduce the risk of making a loss.

Journal

It is important that you maintain a journal and not a digital diary. You must have a hard copy of all the notes that you take down. Always make note of any information that you wish to refer to before you buy or sell stock in the market. This information will be helpful in the future. It is important to look at this information when you make an investment. Keep the journal in a safe place and refer to the information in the journal every now and then to assess when it is the right time for you to buy or sell penny stocks.

Now that you have an idea of what Penny stocks trading is, let us understand how you should start trading. You can either start trading with actual money or begin with paper trading. Remember, that you should only use your money to trade or invest in Penny stocks once you are sure of the strategies and the process to follow.:

Chapter 3

Paper Trading

Before you begin paper trading, you must ensure that you have all the requirements in place. You must have a reliable computer and fast Internet connection. You also need to have suitable software we can record your paper trading results. You must wake up much before the market opens that you can conduct your research about the different stocks. The penny stock market usually opens at 9:30 a.m. You should use the software to go over the market and look for any new information of filing about different businesses. If there are any companies that have released press releases or newsletters about the stocks, place those stocks in your watchlist for that day. You can also make a watchlist to assess the trends so that you can track the progression or regression of a stock that you have selected.

You should now create a watch list for yourself. This list should contain all the stocks that you want to trade in or are already holding. Ensure that this list only includes those stocks that you want to track. Once the market opens you will not have the time to add more stocks to your list. You should be prepared with the list of stocks before the bell goes off. The rates of the penny stocks will fluctuate when the market opens, so wait for them to settle down. Do not be over excited about the fluctuation, and invest in the wrong stock.

When you are tracking the market, ensure that the supply of the stocks that you are looking for are reducing in number. If the supply increases, you should remove the stock from your list. Ensure that no company has filed the S-8 form. If a company has filed this form to the stock exchange commission, it is an indication that they want to increase the number of shares in the market. If the supply increases, the demand for that stock will decrease. You should also check some press releases of the company to ensure that there is no news about the stock. When you follow these steps, you can eliminate the less attractive stocks on your list. When the market opens, you should watch all the stocks in your list and see if your predictions are correct. Verify if people are purchasing the stocks on your list.

You should also check if the number of people selling the stock is less than the number of people buying stock. This is an indication that the price of the stock will go up. That said, if there is a large gap between the ask price and the bid price, you should move away from that stock. Most investors continue to hold onto that stock even when the difference is big, which is where they are wrong. The price of the stock will not increase if the difference is huge. In some situations where the number of sellers is more than the number of buyers, some buyers will opt out of the stock. This will help the seller meet the ideal buyers.

You should always make a note of the number of shares you want to buy on a given day. You should also write the price you are willing to pay against each stock or share. If you are unsure of the number of shares you can afford to purchase, use the following formula:

(Market capital on a given day)/(Ask Price of a stock)

If you have listed a profit percentage limit, you should only sell your stocks when you know you can meet or exceed that limit. Do not be greedy, instead, be patient and wait for the stock price to the increase or decrease. Once you identify the outcomes, add them to your paper trading portfolio.

Repeat this process for a few more days or months to see how you are doing. Make note of your progress and see how you can improve your profits or what you can do better.

Having said that, people struggle to sell stocks at a price they want to. They believe that the price of the stock will continuously increase until it reaches its highest price, and they wait for that to happen before they sell the stock. You should sell a stock the minute it reaches your estimated price and exit the market. A few extra points will not make a huge difference to the profit you earn.

Let us look at some steps you need to follow to invest real money in Penny stocks:

1. You should always meet every requirement, especially the legal requirements. Go through the instruction manual, and

ensure that you understand everything that is to learn about penny stock trading.

2. Now, sign up to an online brokering company and hire a broker. Fund the broker account with cash. You can use Fidelity, Scot trade or E-Trade.

3. Follow all the steps mentioned in paper trading, except that you will now need to invest real money.

4. Set the investment amount.

It is important that you identify the investment amount since you must know how much you can invest in a penny stock. Make sure that you have the right figure, since you will use this amount to buy stocks that are worth your capital. This amount is the initial investment, and you may need to invest more as you go ahead. So, always split the entire investment amount into an initial figure and a pump in figure. For example, if you have $1000, split the amount so you invest $700 now and $300 if needed in the future.

How to Buy Penny Stocks at the Lowest Price

An ask is the real time lowest price at which a person can sell a stock while the bid price is the highest price at which a person can buy the stock. It is important that you understand these terms well. When a seller is placing stock on the share market, he will mark an ask price against that stock. You should ensure that your bid is at least 10% more than the ask price. This is applicable in a highly competitive trade where the demand of stock will surpass supply of stock. You should always set the entry point with your bid price. Make sure you quote the correct bid price since you cannot make a modification to that price. It is important that you do not place a big on a stock that your broker has advised you not to invest in.

If the price of a penny stock is higher than 50% of the actual price, you should avoid purchasing that stock since you are only purchasing a stock whose price is suddenly increasing. Most penny stocks have very high prices when the market opens, and the prices fluctuate constantly. It is always a good idea to purchase a stock at least 30 minutes after the market has opened. You should use your past experience to identify when to purchase a stock and when to sell a stock.

If you are serious about penny stock trading, then you need to take the advice mentioned above carefully. It is important for you to understand how and when you can buy a stock at the lowest price. Regardless of whether you are an amateur or not, never jump in without any experience. The stock market is not forgiving place, and you cannot win on beginners' luck. You should spend some time to understand the market, the different stocks and also assess the trend of the market and stocks. You should then spend some time to understand the companies issuing the stocks to see how they fare in the market. When you have identified the trend of the stock, you can place a bid for that stock at the right ask price. Even if the ask price is lower than your bid; you should not worry about it. You must understand that the price of a penny stock is volatile and fluctuates throughout the day, so make use of that volatility to make a profit. You should sell the stock the minute you believe that the stock has reached the highest price:

Chapter 4

Penny Stock Trading Techniques

If the price of the penny stock is going up, you should exit your position. When the price of a stock goes up, it means that there are numerous buyers waiting to purchase that stock. If you constantly wait for the prices to reduce, you will need to buy the stocks from shareholders who want to exit the market because of the dip in the prices. This means that it is a good idea to sell the stocks earlier to ensure that you match the bid price. This price will not be the price that the seller quotes but is the price that you quote. It is important to remember to buy early and sell early.

Make sure that you do not buy or sell too early. You should wait until the market is fully operational before you buy a stock. If you are in a hurry to buy stocks the minute the market opens, you will not earn a profit. Make sure you time your purchases carefully. As an amateur, you may do the wrong thing when you start trading. This will, however, help you learn what not to do in the future. All your experiences will educate you on what is the right thing to do when you trade in the stock market.

It is a good idea to exit your position in the first ten minutes since this is the only time when the interest is the highest. Experts recommend that you take advantage of this since many companies release information about the stocks of the company when most investors are asleep. This will create a commotion in the market on the following day when the market opens. If you have paid attention to the market, you will note that the position of a penny stock changes rapidly during the first five days. You should try to exit the position before the market closes on the fifth day. This is the only way you can secure your profits. You should not be caught holding a large volume of stocks at the end of the fifth day. If you want to stay at the top of this trade, you must ensure that you follow the hit and run strategy.

If you consider these points when you begin penny stock trading, you can be slightly successful in trading. Having said that, you must conduct further research to learn more about the companies before you trade in their stock. This is the only way you can make more profit when you trade.

When it comes to the stock market, you will come across different types of traders who actively participate in the buying and selling of stocks. It is important that you look at the different techniques and then decide on the technique that works best for you.

Contrarian Trading

Let us first look at the concept of contrarian trading. This concept or trading technique was popularized by Warren Buffet and has existed for quite some time now. It is a unique concept that amuses most traders, both amateurs and experts.

In this technique, the trader is required to always behave or act in the opposite way. They will never do what every other trader is doing but will do the exact opposite. Most investors follow the rules of different forms of trading, and also set some rules for themselves based on their experiences.

If the market is crashing and the condition is bad, most investors will panic and begin to sell their stock. A contrarian trader will instead begin buying shares in the market. This means that the trader is not worried about the change in the prices and is not going to panic. He will take advantage of the situation and will purchase more stocks. At the end, he can accumulate many stocks.

If the prices of stocks increase, investors will begin to purchase new stocks and accumulate them. A contrarian will then be keen to get rid of all the stocks in his account. He can make a profit since he will sell the stocks he has at a high price and would have bought them at a low price.

Pros of Contrarian Trading

The advantage of this form of trading is that it will give the investor an opportunity to maximize his profits by capitalizing the volatility of the stocks and the market. He will benefit from the volatility. A contrarian can buy stocks at low prices and sell them at a higher price, if not the best price, and still make a profit. A contrarian knows that he cannot be greedy and will ensure that he knows when he should sell and when he should buy.

Another advantage of this method of trading is that you can check the balance of the market. So, when people are selling and panicking about the dip in the prices, you as a contrarian trader can maintain the balance of the market by purchasing the shares. It is difficult if there are only sellers and no buyers in the market. You can put an end to this by becoming a contrarian trader.

Cons of Contrarian Trading

Contrarian trading will come with its set of disadvantages or cons. It is important to understand these before you choose to become a contrarian trader.

The first issue is that people may sell their stocks because of some inside information that they may have received. It could be that the company is not doing well which will reduce the value of the stocks. It is during these times that you should analyze the stocks carefully before you choose to buy the stock. Another disadvantage of this method is that you must hold onto a stock until the price of the stock goes up before you sell it. You should know when to get rid of stocks, so you make a profit.

Now that you know both the advantages and disadvantages of this form of trading, you can make an informed decision about whether you want to use this method or not.

Fundamentals Trading

Let us now look at fundamentals trading. When a company chooses to go public, it will quote some shares in the share market. When the company does this, it will need to declare the financial details in the market. These details will help a trader assess the firm and decide if they should invest in the stocks. You can check the financial details of the company at any point, but it is important to remember that a company only releases the reports at the end of every quarter. You only need to go to their website and check the details. The idea behind using this form of trading is that you will make decisions on the basis of the financial health of the company. You will perform an analysis to understand how the company is working. Since there are numerous aspects that you must look at when you perform this type of trading you can take the help of a friend or a broker. We will cover the financial analysis techniques that you must perform in the following chapter. If you wish to become a financial trader, it is important that you perform that analysis first.

Pros of Fundamental Trading

Like every form of trading, fundamental trading also has a list of pros and cons that may appeal to some traders. Fundamental trading will help you assess whether the company is operating peacefully. You can assess if there are any internal troubles at the company. To learn more about the financial health of the company, you only need to visit the website and look at their financial statements. This will not take too long, and when you know how to read these statements, you can gather information about the company in no time. Another advantage of this technique is that you can assess the trend of the stock. You will know which stock will move slowly. If you are interested in a long-term investment, you should choose to invest in a company that is financially sound. So, use the financial statements of the company to help you decide if you should invest in their stocks or not. This is a reverse pro and will help you save enough time and money.

Cons of Fundamental Trading

Fundamental trading is a very good form of trading since you will make informed decisions about your business. Having said that, you should consider fundamental trading only if you want to hold onto these stocks for a long period. You should never use this form of trading if you want to buy and sell stocks quickly. Having said that, you should not write this form of trading off completely. You can use the information about the company to invest in strong stocks. Another disadvantage is that this method is time consuming. You will need to go through every detail mentioned in the financial statement and understand the numbers before you decide. Even if you know how to read financial statements, it may take some time for you to analyze the numbers. The fundamental analysis you perform does not look at human emotions or herd mentality. It is for this reason that you cannot be both a fundamentalist and a contrarian at the same time. You can never be certain if the people around you are buying the stocks, and you may end up with more of one kind of stock.

Technical Trading

The last form of trading is called technical trading. This method is very different from the above types of trading. In this method, you do not worry about what is happening within the firm and do not care about the financial statements. You only worry about the trend that the company's stock is following. This trend will help you establish if the price of a stock is rising or falling. You are only studying the pattern that the stock will follow, and you can do this by looking at the price of the stocks. You can see the trend to assess when the price of the stock will fall, rise or crash. You should place all this information on the graph and look for a pattern. This pattern will tell you where the stock will head next, and whether the price will rise or fall. You will also learn if the stock is predictable and will stick to the trend that you have identified. This is the only way you can assess if the stock is good or not. Technical trading refers to looking at the patterns of the prices of stocks and using that pattern to make an informed decision. This will help you understand how the stock is functioning in the market. You may need to look at the data for a month, five months, a year or more to understand the trend of the stock. You can obtain this information from their reports. The company also publishes this information on the website, and the trading company you choose will have the information readily available for you. You can also choose how the prices will change during the year by looking at the graph.

We will cover the process of technical analysis in detail in the following chapter. This will help you understand how to create a trend and what components of the trend you should look at.

Pros of Technical Trading

There are numerous advantages to using this form of trading. You can establish a proper trend using the data and graphs at your disposal. This will help you assess how the stock will move in the market. The basic assumption is that the stock will always follow a pre-established trend. The price of the stock will rise and fall in the same way that it did in the past. For example, if the price of a stock issued by Apple rises during the middle of the month and falls at the end of the month, you know that you should buy the stock at the end of the month and sell it in the middle of the succeeding month. You can establish a pattern in the same way for every stock that you are interested in. Another advantage is that you do not have to spend too much time trying to understand the company. You do not have to worry about the finances or analyze the financial statements shared by the company. You only have to identify the pattern that the stock will follow in the market. You must, however, learn to interpret the graphs correctly. This is the only way to understand the trend that the stock will follow.

Cons of Technical Trading

There are some disadvantages of using this form of trading. The first disadvantage is that this technique relies heavily on the trends that the stock follows. It does not look at the financial health of the company. This means that you may end up investing in a stock issued by a company that is doing badly in the market. If you continue to hold onto that stock, you will not make a profit once the news about the stock comes out. Another issue with this method is that the graphs do not always show the right trends. It will become impossible or you to predict the mentality of the crowd. There are millions of investors in the market, and it will be hard for you to decide if these investors will stick to a specific trend or will choose to do their own thing. It is for this reason that you should not focus heavily on trends.

These are the different trading techniques you can use when you enter the stock market. You should understand the pros and cons of every method. This is the only way you can choose the right method for you.

Chapter 5

Penny Stock Analysis Techniques

It is important that you analyze stocks well before you invest in them. You will need to look at these stocks through different lenses to understand if they are good investments. This chapter will list some of the best types of analysis that will help you make the right decisions when it comes to investing in a penny stock.

Fundamental Analysis

When you invest in a penny stock, you will be investing in a company. It is important that you understand the financial health of that company before you make the investment. You should collect enough information and go through the right documents that will help you make the right decisions about the investment.

Income Statement

You should use the income statement that you receive every month from the company to understand where the company makes its money. The income statement has information about both the operating and non-operating incomes. The company makes an operating income when it sells the products or services that it manufactures or produces. So, it is a direct result of the work that they do which helps them earn their income. Non-operating income, on the other hand, refers to the amount that the company earns other than selling their products and services. A company can earn a non-operating income by selling some of its possessions like televisions, furniture, etc. If you spot anything unusual in the company's non-operating income, it may indicate a financial crisis. So, investigate before you make an investment in a stock from that company.

Balance Sheet

A balance sheet is a common financial document that every company must maintain to understand and showcase the health of their company. The balance sheet is used to record every transaction of the company including their debts, assets and liabilities. When you go through the balance sheet, you should check if the company has the right assets to balance out the liabilities. If they do not have a balance between the assets and the liabilities, it means that their stocks will not work well in the market. On other hand, if the company has too many assets and very few liabilities then it is a good company to invest in. Remember that the companies always disclose their balances sheets every quarter. So, make sure that you go through all of them. Apart from looking at these factors, you should also check for numerous other aspects in the balance sheet. You should look at the earnings growth ratio of the company since that will help you predict if the value or the price of the stock will increase in the future.

Next, look at the price to earnings ratio. This ratio will give you an idea of the stock of the company is good. Calculate this ratio based on the current price of the share and divide that figure by the total earnings of the company. This will give you the price to earnings ratio. For example, if the price of the stock is $100 and the earnings per share is $5, then the price to earnings ratio is 20%. The stock is not a great investment since the price to earnings ratio is less than the earnings per share. Remember that the stock is said to be good if the price to earnings ratio is high.

You should also look at the dividends that company offers its shareholders. A dividend will indicate if the business is worth investing in or not. If the company pays a continuous dividend, at a constant rate, you can consider investing in the stocks of that company.

Let us now look at some of the fundamental aspects that you should look at in the balance sheet.

Earnings

Earnings refer to the income of the company. It is obvious that the company will have some incoming money. This money will be generated due to the company's functioning. You have to look at the inflow of money and see how much they are making. You want the correct value here and must be sure of the amount that is earned quarterly. You have to calculate the earnings per share and see if the value of the company is good. The earnings per share should always be on a higher side.

Profits

The next thing to check is the profits of the company. You have to see if there are any debts and the assets that they possess. You have to subtract the two and the remaining value is the profit or the loss. It is a debt free company then there will be no problem. The company will be quite a good choice to invest in. you have to calculate the net profit which can be arrived at by using the formula net profit/ revenue earned. If you get a large margin of profit, then it means that the company is being operated optimally and they are well aware of utilizing their budget. Such a company makes for a good investment choice.

Return on Equity

Return on equity is believed to be the most important thing to account for in a company's reports. You have to calculate it and understand what the company's true value is. Return on equity does not take into consideration the per share value, which makes it a great tool to use and understand the company's true worth. The return on investment can be calculated by dividing net income by shareholders equity. That will give you the return on equity, which will tell you whether or not the company is a good choice.

PE Ratio

The PE ratio is better known as the price to earnings ratio. This is to determine whether the share is listed at a good price in the market. It can be calculated by dividing the market value of the share by earnings per share. That will give you an idea of what the price to earnings ratio is. The PE ratio will help you determine the value of the company in terms of its growth and help you understand whether it really is a good company to invest with.

Price to Book Value

The price to book value refers to the actual value of the stock as compared to its book value. It can be calculated by dividing the current share price with the book value for share. That will give you a good idea of the price to book value. The ratio will tell you if you are over paying for the stock and if you need to pay lesser for it.

These form the different things that you must look at and arrive at an appropriate value that you can attach to the company. This value is what you have to use to know the company's worth. You then compare it with the market value and see if the stock has been valued at its true worth. Sometimes, you will stumble across over valued stocks. These can be risky to invest in as any time their prices may fall and your investment will be in danger. So, stick to the undervalued stocks and hold on to them until the time is right to dispose them off.

Cash Flow Statement

Cashflow statements include information about the total cash that is flowing in and out of the company. The cashflow statement will talk about the different incomes and the expenses of the company. You will understand if the company is doing well using that information. This statement is a great tool to use when you want to understand the financial health of the company.

There are a few other legal papers that you should go through to understand the financial health of the company. If you think the company is doing well, then you can invest in it. Having said that, it is important that you invest in the company only when you go through the technical details.

To complete the fundamental analysis, you should check if the company is managed well by the board. The board members make all the decisions about a company. Since they run the business, it is important that you verify if the business is operating peacefully. You can also check if there are any issues internally. Always stay away from businesses where the members constantly fight and never make a unanimous decision.

As discussed, fundamental trading will refer to the process of looking at the health of the company. This form of trading will require you to look at how the company is faring financially. You should assess the different assets and liabilities that the company holds and decide if it is the right place to make an investment. You must perform this analysis in the right manner so you can obtain the desired results.

The best way to perform this analysis is to read the quarterly and annual financial reports of the company. This will help you gather a clear idea about the financial health of the company. You will also know what type of company you are going to invest in. There are a few reasons why people choose to use this type of analysis to understand if a stock is performing well in the market. The first is to know if the market is pricing the stocks correctly or not. If the market is not pricing the stocks correctly, you know that there will be a correction methodology applied to the stocks. The stock exchange can also list the price of stocks incorrectly. This will make it hard for you to assess the financial health of the company. If the prices are incorrect, you can choose to invest in a stock that is undervalued. This is a gamble since you do not know if a correction will be applied to that price.

Make sure that you look at the true value of a stock and compare that value with the value in the market. If the prices match, then the stock has been priced correctly in the market. Otherwise, the stock has either been undervalued or overvalued. If the price is undervalued it is a good investment opportunity.

Technical Analysis

You should also perform a technical analysis to assess if the company is doing well. This analysis will deal with understanding the trends of the stock and also obtain information about the past trends of the stock. You must go through the trends and understand them well before you invest in the stock. There are different types of trends that you should look at before you invest in the stock.

If you do not know how to check for the trend, you can use a computer that will chart an algorithm or use a software. These tools will give you more information about the prices of the stock. The idea is to look at the demand and supply of the stock. As mentioned earlier, the price of the stock will increase if there is a higher demand and a low supply. So, you should check if the price of the overall demand of that stock is low or high. If you only look for movements in the volumes, you should know how to interpret that trend correctly. You can develop a comprehensive graph that will showcase the prices of the stocks clearly. You should understand every component of that graph and study it well to assess where there is a price fluctuation. You should also check if the company you are looking at is a good investment for you or not.

It is difficult to assess the trend when you start off with this type of analysis. You cannot expect to assess the trend of a stock immediately, but if you practice regularly, you will know what your options are and can make the right decisions. There are numerous tools and software available on the Internet that you can use to understand the technical aspects of the company. You can also compare two or more stocks from different companies to obtain a comprehensive analysis. You can then use that analysis to choose the stock that you want to invest in.

Direction

The first thing you must do is to look at the direction in which the price of the stock is moving. A stock will move in the same direction that it usually moves in, either up or down. If you stock moves up or down in regular intervals, it is a good idea to invest in that stock. A balanced stock is a great investment. If the stock you want to invest in has reached the peak point, you should not invest in it. The price will start to fall down. So, you will take a risk if you do invest in a stock that has reached the peak point. If the stock has reached its low point, there are chances that the price will increase. So, it is best to invest in such a stock to ensure that you earn profits. Having said that, you must remember that none of these assumptions may be true. So, it is difficult to generalize. Make note of the graphs and observe them to understand the behavior of prices.

Speed

The next thing to look at is to check the speed at which different stocks move. The stocks will either move up or down in a specific speed, and this speed will determine if the price of the stock will move up or down, and how fast it will reach the extreme point. You can also draw points on the graph to represent the waves which will help you read this graph better and also understand if there is trend that is occurring. Let us assume that the points or waves one and four overlap. This means that the stock is going through a phase where the stock will experience similar values. People wait out this phase and see if the price will settle down. If you see that the price of a stock has moved up too high, then you should understand that this price would also fall or decrease. This trend will help you assess the volatility of the stock.

Distance

Finally, you should also look at the distance that the stock has covered in the market. The stock can continue to break all records and maintain the price. This will only happen when good news about the company breaks out. You will see that the stock will continue to move higher and higher and will then stagnate at the highest point. A stock can also reach its all-time low. This will only happen when some unfavorable news about the company has broken out, and the price of this stock will decrease.

Apart from these aspects, there are other things that you should look into to assess the general trend that this stock will follow. You can collect this information on a monthly basis that will tell you about the rise or dip of the stock. It is important that you understand this information and predict the stocks well. It is important to remember that fundamental and technical analysis is on different planes, and they never converge. It means that a fundamental analyst will not necessarily have the right knowledge about technical analysis and vice versa. If you want to understand how the company you want to invest in functions, you should indulge in these types:

Chapter 6

Myths about Penny Stocks

There are numerous myths that surround penny stocks, and it is important that you understand them and separate them from the facts so you can make informed decisions when you want to invest in penny stocks. Let us debunk some myths that surround penny stocks.

It is not easy to buy and sell these stocks

People believe that it is difficult to trade in penny stocks, and some believe that you should know how penny stocks work and function before you invest in them. This is, however, only a misconception. It is true that penny stocks are elusive, and it is hard to understand them. Having said that, if you know how you can trade in those stocks and know everything you need to know about paper trading, then you will make enough profits. You only have to understand the function of penny stocks and you will be good to go.

Big companies were once penny

People believe that companies like Google and Microsoft were once trading only in penny stocks. These companies are now billion-dollar companies. This is, however, not true. Not every company goes from listing penny stocks to regular stocks in the market. If this company is big, they will automatically list their shares in the market with a big value. A penny stock is small for a small company, especially those companies with small market capitals. This does not mean that the stocks from that company cannot be traded in large volumes. There is no limit on the number of buyers and sellers for a stock. If the stock is very popular now, investors will begin to invest in the market regardless of whether it is a small company or not.

Penny stocks are frauds

Numerous investors believe that penny stocks are fraudulent stocks. They are under this impression since the price of penny stocks is low, and some of them move very slowly. Some investors are suspicious about penny stocks since there are very low volumes of these stocks available in the market. It is never a good idea to think this way. The stock market encourages all forms of stocks. Therefore, it does not matter if the business is big or small for it to list stocks in the market. There can be some frauds in the market, but the presence will be very small.

Prices won't dip further

Never make the mistake of thinking that the price of a penny stock will not dip in the future even if it is doing well at the moment. There is no lower limit for the price of a stock, and the price may constantly dip until the stock is removed from the stock market list. So, never think that the price cannot drop. If you know that the company is good, and even if there is a dip in the price now it can increase in the future, you should continue to hold or invest in that stock. That being said, if you are not very confident, you should ensure that you steer clear of that stock.

Prices surely rise up

If the price of a stock has decreased, there is no way to tell with certainty that the prices will rise again. The price of a penny stock, or any stock in the market, is dependent on the demand for that stock and the supply. So, do not hold onto a stock for too long if it is not doing well in the market. If the price has not increased, you should get rid of that stock immediately.

Penny stocks are safe bets

Many people will tell you that it is a good idea to invest in penny stocks since they are safe. There are, however, many risks to investing in penny stocks. You must understand the different risks and invest when you know how to minimize that risk. The stock market is risky, and this means that any investment that you make in the market is a risky investment. So, you cannot assume that penny stocks are a safe bet. You must identify the stocks that are the right investments and stick to them. You can only make the right decisions once you study the market, and this can take months or years.

You need to be an insider

Please remember that insider trading is a crime. You cannot use the information you have about the company you are working in to invest in stocks in that company. You should use the information that is made available to you by the company to make the right decisions about your investments. It is difficult to buy stocks since there are high buyer volumes and low seller volumes. You must look for the right opportunity so you can enter the market and invest in the stock. This experience will help you learn more about when it is the right time for you to enter the market when it comes to new stocks.

It is best to invest in unknowns

Never invest in companies that you have never heard about. This may not be a good bet for you. It is always good to fall back upon data and invest in those companies that are doing well in the market. It is never a good idea to invest in a small or new company because there is no information available about that stock. You can never be certain if this company will do well in the market or not. You should never invest in such companies. So, the best thing to do would be to invest in a company that has a good record and is doing well.

I'm better off without them

You should ignore this myth, and not read too much into it. If you want to invest in penny stocks and include them to your portfolio, you should. It is true that penny stocks are low priced shares, but they help you diversify your risk. These stocks can give you better and bigger profits when compared to regular stocks. So, you should not make the mistake of thinking that these stocks are less worthy when compared to other stocks. These stocks are one of the better options to invest in. The profits you make from this will help to expand your profit margin.

There are numerous myths about penny stocks, and it is important that you identify the difference between the truth and lies. It is only when you do this that you can make it big in the world of trading

Chapter 7

How Penny Stocks Prices Vary

In the previous chapter, we looked at the different types of stocks and also learned that there are some stocks that are priced very low but are traded regularly in the stock market. These stocks are influenced by some internal and external factors that increased or decreased the value of the share. A penny stock is slightly easier to predict since the market is different from a regular stock market. Therefore, it is easier for you to trade in penny stocks when compared to regular stocks. That said, you must understand the different factors that influence penny stocks and see how the prices vary.

The prices of penny stocks are often influenced by the demand and supply of stocks and the earnings and assets of the company. This means that if there is a high demand and low supply, the price of the stocks will increase. This is the best time to sell the stocks, so you earn a huge margin. Since we rely only on the demand and supply of the stocks to make a profit, you do not have to necessarily evaluate the market. It is enough for you to evaluate the penny stocks and analyze their trends or movement, so you know when it is the right time to buy or sell stocks.

You should also keep an eye out for any news about the company. This news will tell you if the stock of a company will do well in the future or not. Any changes made to the board of the company or an announcement about the profits or bonuses will change the price of the stock. If the company reports a loss, the price of the penny stock will drastically decrease until it reaches the lowest point. You must understand this trend and identify the pattern based on the news. You can then decide to buy, sell, hold or wait on a penny stock. Let us look at this in further detail.

The Fourth Estate and Penny Stocks

The media plays an important role in acting like a catalyst in the price changes of penny stocks. Any negative news about the company will decrease the price of the stocks until some positive news will increase the price of the stock. This does not always have to happen, so it is a good idea to take a closer look at the data and analyze it before you make a prediction. The trick is to determine whether the news you have received will increase the price of the stock.

You can also subscribe to some news journals that will send you alerts about the stock every now and then. When you read about these stocks regularly, you will gather enough information that you can use to leverage your profits. Always pay attention to the company that issues the penny stocks and ensure that you are aware of how you can interpret this news. One can interpret the news in different ways, and it is important that you understand the news correctly. Otherwise, you will make the wrong decisions for yourself. You should also go through the balance sheet of the company to understand how the money moves in the business. Watch the news regularly to look at the updates. These updates will provide you with the best picks and will help you understand or identify the stock that is better for you.

Let us look at some things to look out for when you want to invest in penny stocks. You should look for this information in the news before you decide.

Insider Buying

If an employee is given some sensitive information about the stocks of a company, and he uses that information to purchase stocks in the company it means that the company is going to do well.

Reverse Mergers

A reverse merger is money in the bank. Some companies in the market only serve the purpose to help a private company go public. This will mean that the ownership of the business is no longer private but is in the hands of the public. A private company has assets that will generate revenue, but with a reverse merger a company that was non-functional in the past will acquire new assets. This will generate revenue, which will affect the price of the stocks.

Survival From Bankruptcy

When a company announces that it is going bankrupt, the stock prices will decrease suddenly. The company may then announce that it planned to avoid this bankruptcy, and this will increase the price of the stock. This is a good time for you to invest in the penny stock of this company since the value of the stock will reach an all-time low before its value increases. Some companies use this technique to influence the price of their stocks.

New Patent

If a penny stock company has requested or obtained a right to a new patent, it means that there will be higher revenue in the future.

Affiliation With A Big Company

It is true that many investors want to associate themselves with big companies. If a well-known company wants to do business with a small penny stock company, it is evident that the company is looking for ways to grow. A big company will always choose its business partners carefully and will only acquire if every checkbox is ticked. This means that you should invest in the small penny stock company.

Quarterly Financial Numbers

Every company releases its financial statements at the end of every quarter. A good quarterly report will increase the price of the stocks since the numbers represent the current situation of the company. This could have happened due to numerous reasons including an increase in the royalty fees, the number of contracts and a higher demand for the products or services offered by the company.

Positive Signs to Look for

Prediction is everything when it comes to trading in penny stocks. You must understand whether the price of a stock has increased or decreased and assess whether the price of the stock is bound to change anytime soon. If the price will fall, you should understand how to react to the change. Let us look at some signs to look for to understand if the stock prices are going to increase.

Precedence

One of the best ways to assess if the price of a stock will rise or fall is to look at historical data. So, look at how the company's management performed in the past to assess whether the price of your stock will rise or fall. The CEO of the company and the management will make this decision. When you check the past records of a company, you will find information about how the company dealt with the changes made to the stocks. You will also learn about any bonus shares that the company may have offered. A company can choose to offer its customers bonus shares that will increase the price of the stock in the market. This is one of the best opportunities to capitalize on and to buy the shares. You can then sell the shares at the highest values.

News

If a company manages to remain in the news in the long run, it is sure to benefit in the stock market. The news about the company's stock is much like advertising the stock of the company. When you watch an advertisement, you want to buy the product because of how the advertisement glorifies that product. In the same way you will want to purchase a share or stock of the company if there is some good news about that company. The news can be regarding the technical or fundamental aspects of the company. This information will make the business remain in the news, and you will benefit from this. Make sure that you tune into any news about the company. Both good news and bad news will change the price of the stocks.

Market Capture

If a company increases its market share, it will clearly indicate that the products of the company are doing well in the market. You can benefit from investing in the stocks of that company, and it is a good idea to buy these stocks at the earliest. The market capture also determines whether there is immense pressure on the company and the competitors. If there is a change in the price of the share of one company, the stock prices of the shares its competitors' will be affected. So, you must see if you want to buy, hold or sell the shares before they are affected further.

Results

When a company announces the results, there will be a change in the share or stock price. If the results are good, there will be an increase in the share price and if the results are bad the stock prices will dip. You should be aware of when the company will announce its results and decide whether you want to wait, buy, hold or sell the stock that you may have invested in.

Small vs. Big

When it comes to small shares, you should try to invest in those offered by large companies since they are better than small companies on any given day. So, look for a multi-million-dollar company, and see if the share price is lower when compared to a small company whose share prices are more. A contrarian trader will choose the latter, but you should decide based on your investment profile. With the former it is easy to predict how the stock will impact the market. So, you will know how to determine which stock to invest in based on the trend of the company, stock and the market.

High Low Patterns

People believe that if a stock is dipping, it will continue to dip, and a stock that is rising will continue to rise. That said, the contraction belief says that the stock on the rise will dip while a stock that is dipping will rise. These are two different ways of looking at the stock market, and you cannot determine that one method is incorrect. That being said, it is important that you always look for the highest lows and highest highs for every stock. If a stock dips below the one year low, then the stock is in trouble and will not move anywhere. If the stock has hit the highest mark, then it is one of the best stocks to invest in. It is a good idea to immediately invest in that stock.

Apart from these signs, you should also look for the volume and money movements. These have been covered in detail later in the book

Chapter 8

How To Minimize Risk

As mentioned earlier, it is quite risky to trade in penny stocks since there is not too much information available about this stock. Your best shot is to use the information that has come out in the news or media. This will mean that you need to find different ways to reduce the risk as much as possible. If you want to minimize the risk, you should know how to identify common traps that most penny stock investors find themselves in.

Message Boards

There are stock cons, like comic cons, that influence numerous buyers and sellers to trade in stocks. These buyers and sellers will pretend to advise you in a manner that will leave you wanting to invest in that stock. You will not know if you are being cheated. These people include bashers and pumpers. A basher is someone who will convince you that the stock you have invested in is bad and convince you to sell that stock. They are duping you. A pumper, on the other hand, will tell you that a stock is doing well in the market, and convince you to buy those stocks. When they know that they have convinced enough people to buy that stock, they will create a false demand that will increase the price of the stock in the market. They will then sell those shares at a high rate to make a profit. It is for this reason that you must be aware of these tricks. You can use message boards to do this. Most websites have message boards that will shed some light on stocks and also provide enough information about the stock. There will be some people who will tell you to invest in a specific stock because of some details. You will probably invest in that stock but will not gain too much profit, which will mean that you should start from beginning. So, you should stay away from these cons as much as you can, so you only trust reliable sources to pick the stock you want to invest in.

Stock Promoting E-Mails And Faxes

Some so-called experts will send you faxes or emails to tell you about the market and also about the way the prices are rising and falling. It is a good idea to avoid acting upon this information and decide based on research. The emails or faxes will look like they come from reliable sources but on investigation you will notice that the information is false. The people sending you this information are often frauds and they are doing this only to increase the price of a penny stock. You will know better than to indulge in believing these facts and emails.

Group Runs

It is very tricky to understand group runs since these groups consist of organized groups of traders who will come together and also buy the stocks that have a low volume. This will attract attention from the other investors in the market. If the prices shoot up because of this demand, these groups will sell the shares at a high price and leave the last person to purchase these shares at a high price. This will lead to a loss for the person purchasing these stocks. You can invest in these stocks, but you will need to be fast. Make sure that you know exactly when to buy and purchase such stocks.

Average News

People do not like to average, and any average news will not help you make a profit in the market. Averages do lead to returns. Therefore, you should make sure that the news is accurate before you invest in the penny stock. Never settle for a company that is not great since that will affect your profits. Your money is of great value to you, so you must invest it carefully in the market.

Too Much News

Some companies have too many press releases and the information from these releases will influence the prices of penny stocks. You should, therefore, approach these stocks with great caution. If you are an amateur, you should work on gathering more information about penny stocks and see whether the business is only using these press releases to increase the prices of the stocks. An experienced trader will never invest in such stocks and you should never too.

S-8 Filing

You should always keep a track of whether a company is filing the S-8 document to the Stock Exchange Committee. This document will tell the stock exchange that the company is going to increase the number of shares in the market. If you see that a company has filed this report, you should avoid investing in that company since the supply is now high

Chapter 9

Dos and Don'ts of Penny Stocks

This chapter sheds some light on the different things you should do and not do when it comes to investing in penny stocks. It is important that you invest in the right stocks to improve your profits.

Things To Do

Let us look at some things that you can do with penny stocks.

Do make use of risk capital

Risk capital is the amount of money you are willing to risk. If you think you have some money that will go to waste, then you should use that as the capital to invest in penny stocks. You should never worry if the stocks are at a low price or if they are going bad. It is important that you are prepared for the losses since this will help you make the right moves. It is important that you make use of money that belongs to you. Make sure that you invest in the right stocks.

Do your research

It is important that you always conduct thorough research. If you look at a message board and are aware that there is a specific stock that is doing well in the market, conduct research and obtain the information about that stock. Never invest in a stock blindly. There is going to be some information that will mislead you and throw you off. So, you must conduct research on the stock before you make an investment in the stock. Make sure that you perform both a fundamental and technical analysis to ensure that you obtain the right information about the stock.

Do sell fast

It is important that you always sell your penny stocks fast. Penny stocks are often bought and sold on the same day. This will give you a chance to make an immediate profit. When you take lesser time to make a profit, your confidence in investing in penny stocks will increase. Therefore, it is important that you are quick about making the right purchase or sale. This will seem slightly daunting at first, but you will get better with experience and you can make the right decisions.

Do look for high volumes

It is important that you always look for high volume trades. The numbers should always look right. The numbers should always be accurate, right up to the decimal point. If you invest in these stocks, you will certainly make a profit. Make sure that you always look at those stocks with a higher volume and invest in them. This is the only way that you can make the right trade. If you see that a stock is doing well in the market, you can place a call on that stock. If the stock continues to move at a good price, then you should sell it so you can make a profit.

Do cut loses

Make sure that you reduce your losses. You may lose out on some capital when you sell your stocks short. It is only when you try to maintain a positive approach towards your stocks that you can earn from them. Always make smart investments and ensure that you stay away from the stocks that will lead to losses.

Don't make these Mistakes

Let us now look at some things you should not do when you choose to invest in penny stocks.

Don't get attached

It is important that you do not get attached to the stocks that you invest in. If you get emotionally attached to the company you invest in and only invest in those stocks because you like the company, you will make some mistakes. These mistakes can lead to losses, and this is not what you want to achieve with the investments that you make. If the company you are investing in is good, then you should invest in it because you know the stocks will pay you. Never invest in stocks and simply sit on them because you like the company. Remember that the money you invest in those stocks can be used in better places.

Don't read too much

It is true that you should conduct thorough research before you invest in a penny stock. That being said, if you do read too much you will be confused. If you want to gather the right information, you should stick to one good book about the topic. This is the only way you can obtain the right information about the stocks. This book has the right information about penny stocks, and if you are an amateur, you can learn how to invest in penny stocks using the information in this book. Make sure that you read all the necessary information before you invest in penny stocks. People make the mistake of trusting emails and faxes from people or listen to what someone around them may say. This information will only misguide you and you will invest in the wrong stocks.

Don't short

Avoid selling your penny stocks short because that will create a loss magnet. If you sell a stock short because you do not want to stick with it, you will continue to do the same. The small losses will accumulate and will become a big loss for you. You need to be very careful and ensure that you do not develop the incorrect habits. Make sure that you always sell your stocks short only if there is nothing else that you can do with them.

Don't be unreasonable

Never make unreasonable expectations about your investments. This is the only way you can diversify your risks. Do not expect to see some results overnight. If you want to invest your money today, you should wait for a month or two before you see the profits. You will only make small profits before the amount increases to thousands. You have to remain patient and ensure that you are in no rush to see some results. You cannot expect to see results very soon.

Don't copy

Never copy the investment decisions that someone else has made. Your investment plan will be different from others. So, make sure that you do not pick a stock simply because another person has picked that stock to invest in. The strategies that work for another person will not necessarily work for you.

Chapter 10

Methods Used to
Predict Trading

Let us look at some methods you can use to predict the trends that a penny stock or any stock in the market will follow.

Following Trend

The easiest and commonly used method to assess stocks is the trend following method. Experts say that following the trend of the stock is the best way to predict the fate of that stock. The assumption made when using this method is that the stocks that are rising will fall and those that are falling will still continue to fall. When you use this method, you can identify the trend and invest in those stocks that will generate a profit. This technique does not always work but it is a good technique to adopt in most cases.

Contrarian Trading

Many expert traders use the contrarian trading method to make profits in the stock market. In this way of thinking, you do not look at the trends of the market. The traders will invest in those stocks that are falling and sell the stocks that are rising. Experts believe that this is one of the best ways to judge the stocks in the market. You must remember that this method will only work for you if you know how to select the right stocks.

Candlesticks

You can also use statistical methods, like candlesticks, to predict the stock trends. You must place candlesticks on a graph with a specific pattern in mind. You should then look at the highest point and the lowest point of that stock. Identify the path of the stock and mark the midpoint. You should also mark the different prices that the stock will hit. Since this is a statistical method, you will need to perform some calculations before you create the graph. You can take the help of a professional if you are unaware of how to do this.

Price Action Trading

Price action trading is another method that most investors use to help them predict the trend of the market and the stocks. As an investor, it is important for you to understand how the prices of a stock will rise or fall. For this, you will need to look at the monthly or weekly trends of the stocks and predict which ones will rise or fall depending on the data that you have. If the stock rises at the start of the day but slowly falls during the day, you will know whether you should invest in that stock or not. You will know that you should always buy the stock during the day and sell it when the market opens on the following day. You must identify the trend and use that to your benefit.

Range Trading

Range trading refers to the method where you only trade in a predetermined range. You can define this range depending on what your upper limit and lower limit of risk is. You can then choose to trade at any point within that range. For instance, if the lower limit is $5 and the upper limit is $40, the trader will buy and sell the stocks only within that range. They do not worry about the stocks that are priced lower than $5 or higher than $50. The only objective is to stay between the range.

Rebate Trading

Rebate trading is another good trading method to choose from, especially if you are an amateur. This technique uses ECN's to make a trade. In an ECN, you will make an investment and pay some commission towards that investment. The system will then invest your money in the market in the stock that you have chosen. There are many investors like you who will pay a commission towards ECN, and the company will make a profit. This is a very safe method since the ECN will create a large market for you and there will be enough money that can be invested in different stocks.

News Following

As mentioned earlier, it is important that you follow the news about the stock market and trends. As an investor, it is your responsibility to look at all the stocks and understand how each of them is doing in the market. You should always ensure that you maintain a profit when you invest in the market. You should read the company reports, go through their financial statements and see if there is any news about a merger or an acquisition. Make sure that you understand how the company functions and what their products and services are. This will help you make the right decision about whether or not you should invest in the stock.

Swing Trade

This is one of the best techniques to apply when you trade in stocks. This technique will help you identify the trend of the stock successfully. Let us assume that you bought a stock at $1, and the price fell to $0.5. You then decided to sell that stock. Now, if you choose to buy another stock, you will need to buy it at the same rate at which you let go of the previous stock. You can then wait until the price of the stock reaches $5 before you sell it. This will help you make a profit.

Artificial Intelligence

Artificial intelligence is a technique where you give the computer all the numbers and allow it to calculate the required output. All you need to do is feed the right data into the system and allow the computer to give you the required result. The computer will look at the data and assess the stocks. It will then tell you which stock you should invest in. This method is accurate 90 percent of the time. You should try to combine different outputs to assess whether the stock is a good investment or not.

These prediction methods will help you understand how a stock will move when the market opens the following day and throughout the day

Chapter 11

Types Of Brokers

It is important that you always choose the right broker since they are an important part of investing in the stock market. They will help you make the right decisions when you enter the stock market. A broker does not necessarily need to advise you to make the right decisions but will play many other roles.

Regular Brokers

A regular broker is someone whose job is to only buy and sell shares or stocks for you. This is their job requirement and they will not venture into suggesting the right stocks for you to invest in. there are some who are part-time brokers and they will only do as you say. When you hire these brokers, you can start off with investing in the market on the right foot. Regular brokers are not tied to firms, and you can hire them independently. They will charge you a sum for their services rendered to you. Some of these brokers may have been hired to mislead people into making investments that will benefit others. They may suggest some stocks to you. So, before you agree to let them invest in a stock, you should make sure that you conduct research and understand the performance of that stock in the market.

Full Time Brokers

A full-time broker is someone who is hired to take complete care of your investments. These brokers are specialized and have good knowledge about the stock market. They also know when one should invest or sell stocks to make profits. These brokers will tell you how much you should invest in each stock as well. You will need to spend a little more when you choose to invest in a full-time broker since they spend all their time helping you out. These brokers buy the stocks, sell them and also perform the right research to help you invest in the stock market. Most full-time brokers are not interested in investing in penny stocks since the trend is hard to predict. These brokers prefer to invest in large companies since the prices are predictable. Therefore, if you choose to invest only in penny stocks, you should not choose a full-time broker. If you are going to invest in other stocks, you can choose them.

Boiler Room Brokers

A boiler room broker is one who is present only to mislead the public. These brokers are people you should be very careful about and avoid engaging with them. A boiler broker's main job is to draw the suckers and cheat them, and they will do anything to do this. These people know all the tricks of the trade and know how to influence any stock in the market. This will increase the demand for that stock thereby increasing an investor's loss. People dread coming across a boiler room broker and it is very difficult to spot one. These brokers will act like they are interested in giving you the right information but that is not what they want to do.

Online Traders

Online traders are people who work only on websites to help you buy and sell stocks. These brokers can either work in a firm or work independently. They will help you trade your stocks and also give you advice about the stock market. An online trader will prefer that you trade only in predictable stocks since they would have compared the risks. They will charge you a little more when compared to regular brokers, but they will have a lot of experience. If you are a beginner and are looking for a way to invest in stocks, then you should consider these brokers. You must ensure that you differentiate between the honest and fraudulent brokers.

Floor Brokers

A floor broker is someone who will operate only from the base or the floor of the stock exchange. These people will work in the stock exchange and they will take orders from the people and execute those orders. It is hard to identify these brokers and choose the right ones. Most floor brokers do not choose to help you invest in stocks. So, it is best that you avoid looking for a floor broker.

You should look at the different types of brokers and see the type of broker that will suit your needs or requirements best. They will help you invest in the right stocks

Chapter 12

Unavoidable Rules of Day Trading Penny Stocks

You must bear some rules in mind when you choose to invest in penny stocks. Make sure that you understand these well before you invest in the market. You should swear by these rules if you want to make the most from trading in penny stocks. These rules were formulated by experts who bore in mind the way the market changes and operates.

Always stick to your gut

It is important that you set some rules for yourself when you choose to invest in the stock market. You should remember to adhere to those rules when you invest in the market. Never be swayed by any information unless you are certain of your judgment. People often get carried away and purchase stocks that they do not want simply because of something they may have read. If you do this, you will only make a loss. You will probably repeat this in the future too. Make sure that you plan your investments and trust your gut feeling. It is only when you know that you are making the right choice for you that you will be happy with the investment. If your intuition says that you should not purchase a stock, then make sure that you do not, even if it is your best friend telling you to purchase that stock. That being said, your intuition may lead you to purchase a stock that has bad reviews. Do not do this unless you have the right information to back your decision.

Only use money that you are ready to put to risk

It is a gamble when it comes to trading in penny stocks. You will be playing with money that you may or may not want to lose. It is important that you always use funds that you are not emotionally attached to. Do not use the money you need to pay the bills to invest in penny stocks since there is a possibility that you may incur a loss that will leave you in a bind. This will lead to some fear, which will make you a conservative investor, and you will make the smallest investments, which will not give you any profits. If you do wish to invest in penny stocks, make sure that you set some amount aside at the start of every month so you can use that money to invest in the stock. Make sure that you use this money sparingly and are okay with taking a risk with that money. You should understand that there are no guarantees when it comes to trading in the stock market, and you may end up losing more than you earn. You must always look at the positives and negatives of making an investment. A wise investor will ensure that he has calculated the risks before investing in the stock. Therefore, you should do the same if you want to make a profit from your investments.

Educate yourself about the market everyday

It is important that you study the market regularly and keep yourself abreast with the different factors that lead to a change in the market and stocks. You should ask yourself if you have traded in the right stocks when the market closes. This will help you decide which stocks to invest in the following day. If you believe that a book will help you obtain all the information you need to know about penny stocks, then you are wrong. It is important to remember that the market does not stay the same every day. The market will change, and you will be in different situations. You must ensure that you always adjust your purchases based on your experiences. It is important that you make note of everything that is happening in the market and use your experience and knowledge to help you make the right purchases in the future.

Learn from your experience

If you want to make money through penny stock trading, you should learn to own your mistakes, learn from them and become better at investing in penny stocks. The more you learn from your mistakes and your past experiences, the better you will be at making decisions now. You will also find yourself making larger profits. So, do not keep thinking about this and worrying about the stocks. The market will be punishing at times, but you will also make enough profits if you know how to invest. So, do not be overenthusiastic about profits or bog yourself down because of a loss. Make sure that you never repeat a mistake twice. You should anticipate how a situation would impact you, and the only way to do this is for you to learn from your previous experiences.

Be realistic

When you determine the profit percentage that you may make, ensure that you are realistic. If you set a very high percentage, it will mean that you are at a risk of making a loss. Ensure that you are realistic and set the right percentage for yourself. Make sure that you do not underestimate the percentage as well. Experts suggest that you set the percentage to 10% when it comes to daily trading and 20% if you focus on the trends since the latter are easy to determine. You can be certain that you will make some profit if you focus on the trend. Some believe that 10% is too low for a profit, but if you calculate you will see that a 10% profit every day will sum up to a decent amount at the end of the month. Never aim too high since it is a good idea to play safe. If the opportunity presents itself to you, you can release a stock. Never wait on a stock simply because you think the price may change. You can never predict the pattern, and if the opposite happens you will be in trouble.

Be a quick decision maker

Make decisions quickly. When it comes to investing in penny stocks, you must ensure that you are fast. You cannot waste time. This does not mean that you should dive into making a bid without thinking twice. If you always hesitate, you will end up purchasing a penny stock when it is at its highest only to end up making a loss when you sell the stock. You should ensure that you are not the last one standing especially when the demand for the stock increases. Never chase a stock for too long, and this is a dangerous thing to do when the stock market opens. When the market opens, it is hard to know whether the stock will do well or not. If you do not make the right decisions, you will lose more money than you started with.

Keep your funds liquid everyday

When you purchase a stock, you should ensure that you sell that stock on the same day or in a few days. You must ensure that you have liquid assets since you need money to trade in the stock market. You must ensure that you have sufficient money to invest in a good deal. If you do not do this, you will miss out on a great opportunity because you did not have enough money to invest in that stock. Another thing to remember is that most penny stocks show a huge growth in one day, and the prices will decrease by the end of the day. So, make sure that you grab the opportunity while you still have it. Buy and sell the stocks immediately and on the same days because you are unsure of how the stock will function tomorrow.

Be your own boss in making decisions

If you are wise, you will make your decisions. If you want to get some advice, make sure that you do not listen to the advice of a person who is trying to convince you to buy or sell a stock. If you do listen to them, you will be duped. People always have their own interests at heart, so make sure that you know where your interests lie. Always make independent decisions since this is the only way you can make a profit if you invest in penny stocks. If you can be swayed easily based on some information you may have read somewhere on the Internet. You should remember that the prices of penny stocks also keep shifting. Therefore, you must know when to say no and also know what information you should trust. If your broker suggests some stock to you, be cautious and try to understand that stock better. Conduct research and learn if the information that they are providing is right or wrong. Your broker should only help you buy and sell stocks. The same goes for the information on a website. If you believe that it is a good idea to invest in a stock, then you invest in that stock but ensure that you make this decision based on strong data and evidence.

Only go for big news and nothing less

As mentioned earlier, there is some news that people use to influence the stock market. These emails will determine the price of the stock. In reality, this news does not affect the price of stocks, but makes people anticipate that there is something coming, Average news will only give you average returns. It is only the big news that will help you make the largest profit. So, make sure that you are on the lookout for big news, and pounce on that opportunity. If you want to avoid making a mistake when it comes to trading in penny stocks, you should be aware about some mistakes that people often make. The following is a list of some mistakes that people often make.

Mistakes To Avoid

- A common mistake people make it to start at an entry point that is greater than 50 percent. This happens the minute the stock market opens. You should never assume that the prices of stocks would go up. A rapid increase in the price of a stock is short-lived, and before you know what is happening, the price of the stock will fall again. You should always avoid investing in a stock whose price increases in the first few minutes. Always focus on those stocks that make a gradual progress.

- You may want to reduce the trader account balance limits, and to do this you may trade between 30 and 50 percent of your balance.

- Do not read too much into the information you see on message boards or on social media.

- You may want to make a profit of at least 25 percent when you invest in stocks. So, make sure that you do not hold onto a stock for too long after you have made a profit.

- When you buy randomly, you will make a mistake that is similar to purchasing stocks based on the information on message boards. Never blindly trust the information that a colleague, friend or neighbor may give you. Make sure that you always conduct enough research:

Chapter 13

Tips And Tricks For Successful Penny Stocks Trading

There are some tips and tricks that you can keep up your sleeve to help you invest in penny stocks. Let us look at some of them.

Buy Low; Sell High

Make sure that you always buy low and sell high. This is the oldest trick in the book, and it is important that you follow it to the tee. It is only when you do this that you will make large profits in the market. When you buy low and sell high, you will purchase a stock at its lowest value and sell that stock at its highest value. You can determine when the stock will reach its highest value based on some data and methods you use. Ensure that you always act according to the data that you collect and analyze. Many experts recommend that it is a good idea to buy stocks the minute the market opens. Most stocks reach their highest price in the afternoon, and that is when you should sell them.

Scalping

Scalping is a technique that is very popular in the penny stock market. In this technique, you can buy and sell stocks in a few minutes or seconds depending on how fast you are. It is a strange method, but it is one that works wonders in any volatile market. Let us assume that you purchase a stock at 12 PM and dispose it off at 12:02 PM. The buying price of that stock is $3, and the selling price is $5. So, in a matter of two minutes you made a $2 profit per share, and this is a great profit for a scalper. It may not seem like much, but a scalper will do this at least fifteen times a day and make a large cumulative profit. That being said, it is a good idea to choose this type of investment only when you become an expert in the market. If you want to take up this technique, you should have at least a year's worth of experience to help you make the right decisions.

Short Selling

Short selling is a concept that is used in the penny stock market. Short selling refers to when you borrow a stock from the stockholder and sell those stocks to a buyer. You will then wait for the price of the stock to fall before you give the stocks back to the lender. This is one of the best ways to capitalize on the volatility of penny stocks. Having said that, you must make the right decisions about the investments you make and not invest or borrow useless stocks. Make sure that you have a wide margin that will allow you to borrow the stocks. You must have enough capital to support any other investment if things do not work out. It is always a good idea to buy shares back at the earliest if you believe that the price of the stocks will continue to increase.

Money Movement

If you notice a sudden change in the movement of the price and the flow of money in the company, you know that the stock value will increase. If there is a sudden increase in capital in the through external sources or it pumped its profits into its business, then it means that the company wants to expand. This will mean that the stock prices will rise, and it will benefit you as an investor. You must always keep track of the news and make the right decisions.

Volume

If you notice a sudden change in the volume of a stock, it is a good idea to invest in that stock. Sudden ups and downs in the volume will occur only when there is some information about the stocks that is either making people buy or sell the stocks. You should also capitalize on such situations, so you make large profits. According to Timothy Sykes, you should always purchase a penny stock if it is experiencing a high price after one year. This will mostly happen when the company talks about its bonus.

Don't Trust Mails

As mentioned earlier, it is important that you do not trust any emails that come from companies that claim to have enough knowledge about the stocks of other companies. These emails will also suggest the stocks that you should invest in, but the information in those emails is untrue. Companies cannot go through their investors' portfolios and suggest which stocks they should invest in. Even if a company does choose to do this, they may give you a suggestion that will not work for you. So, it is a good idea to avoid these stocks and only invest in those stocks that you have all the information about.

Pattern

It is important to remember that penny stocks and every other stock in the market will follow a pattern. Once you notice this pattern and understand it, you can invest in penny stocks successfully. This pattern has all the information you need about the high and low points of the stocks, and also gather some information on how you can trade between those points. It is important to have the history of the stock with you since it will help you determine the previous trend and also predict the future trend of the stock.

Results

It is important that you always look for companies that are result-oriented. When a company publishes their report, you should check that report and ensure that they are doing well in the market. You must be sure that the company is the right investment choice for you. The results of the data collection should show you that you could make enough profits when you invest in this company. A small company will always aim to sell a large volume of stocks, and if you are impressed with the company and its numbers, you can invest in the stocks of that company. It is important to remember that the results are only published quarterly, and it is extremely important that you look at every result before you invest in a company.

Name

It is true that the name of a company matters a lot when it comes to trading in penny stocks. You must see if the company is well-known and is doing well in the market. If the company is not very important or there are any stories that will change the way the company is viewed, you should not invest in that company. Some people steer clear of such companies. If you are not a fundamentalist and are willing to take on a few risks, you can use technical analysis to help you make the decision. It is, however, important that you learn more about the company before you invest.

Reliable Information

Always focus on reliable sources and read the information there carefully. Make sure that the sources you use are trustworthy. If you get an email, tip or fax that a certain company is 100% reliable, and you will make the right investment choice by investing in the stocks of that company, stop right there. You should never choose to invest in a company simply because of some information that was given to you. You should conduct thorough research to learn if the business you want to invest in is doing well or not. You do not want to end up wasting your money. Therefore, stick to reliable sources and use that information to invest in the right stocks.

Corrections

It is important that you remain patient during a correction. The stock price will drop when a correction is going on, and if you are impatient, you will make a wrong move and will lose on a lot of money. You must look at the status of the company and perform the right calculations to see if the stock is listed at the right price. If a stock is either overpriced or underpriced, it means that the corrections will be made soon. You should prepare for those corrections to be made and not sell the stocks you have in a panic. Follow the news regularly to see if the correction is being made.

Don't hire penny stockbrokers unless you really have to

Another important thing to bear in mind is that you do not hire a broker to invest in penny stocks unless you are in dire need of one. These brokers usually have different fees and also ask for a commission. This will eat into your earnings. Penny stockbrokers will always need to be paid a commission regardless of whether or not you make a profit. So, they will never put in too much effort to ensure that you are always making a profit. Some theories exist that companies try to hire brokers and ask them to convince people to trade in a specific stock even if they are not interested in trading in that stock. If you are easily swayed, you will purchase this stock, which can lead to losses. Try to look for online discounts that will help you trade penny stocks independently. You should avoid depending on your broker to buy and sell your stock.

Don't invest in penny stocks whose trading volume is less than 100000 per day

Ensure that you choose the penny stocks you want to invest in carefully. You should try hard to avoid investing in penny stocks that are low in volume since they will be less liquid. The price per share of these stocks is very low, so it is important that you invest in those stocks that you know are being traded. If the price of the penny stocks begins to decrease, there will be very few people willing to buy those stocks since the volume of those stocks is very low.

Do not invest in penny stocks from the same industry

Remember to diversify your risks regardless of the type of investment you are making. The same holds true for penny stocks. When you invest in a penny stock in the same industry you are increasing the risk. It is a good idea to invest in the same industry, but what will you do if the industry comes crashing down? You will lose the investments you have made. It is for this reason that you should always diversify your risks when you invest in the stock market. If you believe that the IT industry is doing well and you want to invest in the stocks in that industry, you can do so. Having said that, make sure that you do not invest every single penny you own only in that industry.

Focus your attention on company behind the stock

It is true that you should focus on how the stock is doing in the market. Having said that, it is more important to focus on the company that is issuing the stock. You must know if the company you are investing in is working on developing new products, services or technology. You should assess how this will affect the price of the stock, and the best way to do this is to use the fundamental analysis approach and to read the news. These are the best places for you to assess if the company is doing well. If you have some knowledge about the products of the company, then you should perform an analysis to help you understand where the company is heading.

Always be Informed

You must ensure that you are always informed about every occurrence in the stock market. You should go through different publications and resources to gather the necessary information about any penny stock activities.

If you trade in penny stocks in the right way, you will make large profits. Let us look at some tips that will help you increase your profits or yields.:

Chapter 14

Tips To Successfully Trade
In Penny Stocks

Now that you have an idea of the basics of penny stock trading, let us look at some ways to help you trade in penny stocks. These methods will increase your chances of reducing the risks with trading in penny stocks and help you make a profit.

Never focus only on success stories

Rolf Dobelli, in his book 'The Art of Clear Thinking,' talks about habit called the survivor bias. This bias makes it difficult for you to think clearly. It is important that you always think clearly when it comes to threading in Penny stocks. According to Dobelli, this by overestimate are chances of succeeding in are chosen endeavor because we focus only on the possibilities of success more than the possibilities of failure. This basis exacerbated when people rebel those who are dualistic incautious as party pooper, pessimists or failure minded people. People make it sound like it is a mortal sin to be mindful of possible dangers of risks and this mindfulness cannot be forgiven.

This bias only glorifies positivity over realism. Most success, regardless of whether it is in life on penny stock trading, will only be learnt through stories of failure. Think about Thomas Edison's success. He invented a light bulb that changed the way human beings live forever. He could not, however, succeed in his first attempt. He worked on numerous experiments before he succeeded. Thomas Edison said that he did not fail when these experiments didn't work, but learned a different way to invent or create the light bulb. The funny thing is, experts say that the unforgettable lessons that they learnt while trading in Penny stocks were from their failures. This is probably the only reason why people are motivated to do better so they can avoid failure.

If you only focus on success stories, you will overestimate your chances of success. This will blind you, making it difficult for you to look at or identify signals. This will lead to a huge loss of your capital. Having said that, you should never disregard your success stories. In other words, you must have a clear idea or approach and consider you're your successes and failures. For every success that you identify, there will be two or three failure stories to report. It is only when you fail and identify the mistakes in your strategies that you will do better. You should also learn how you could continue to succeed in trading in Penny stocks.

Focus on disclaimers instead of tips

Remember that penny stocks are not bought but sold on most occasions. This means that the demand for Penny stocks is weak. If a business wants an investor to purchase a penny stock, it should advertise that penny stock. The business should also shed some light on the advantages of penny stocks when compared to regular stocks. Most investors choose to buy penny stocks depending on some information they read in a newsletter or email. The issue with these letters and emails is transparency. Timothy Sykes says that these emails and letters are not sincere, and the management or person sending those emails or letters to the investor never expected the investor to succeed. The bottom section of the email should contain a disclaimer and a few tips about how you should trade in the stock.

Most people sending out these emails and letters are paid by companies that have issued penny stocks. The information in these letters or emails about the penny stock will provide good exposure to the public. This will make them want to purchase the stock. Exposure is not everything since the sender is only trying to promote the stock.

When people pay attention to the information in these emails and newsletters, they begin to invest in the penny stock, which will increase the price of that stock. Having said that, the price of a stock does not necessarily have to reach an all-time high price only because of the information in these newsletters or emails. So, how do you identify why there was a sudden increase in the price of the stock? The easiest way to identify whether the information in a newsletter or email is true, is to look for the disclaimer. If you notice that an email does not contain a disclaimer, you should ignore the contents of that email or delete the email immediately because the information in that email is untrue. Stock exchange committee requires that people sending out these emails add a disclaimer at the bottom of that email since this disclaimer will help you understand if there is a conflict of interest. If there is no disclaimer at the end of the email, you can be certain that there is a conflict of interest.

Sykes also mentions that newsletters and emails are often sent to increase the demand of a stock. When an email or newsletter is sent to multiple readers about a specific stock, the users are bound to purchase the stock, which will increase the stock price. These newsletters and emails do not give you tips on when you should sell stock. Even if they give you the information on when you should sell a stock, it will be too late for you to sell so you can make a profit.

Sell Fast

Trading in Penny stocks is different from long term investing. The latter involves a buy and hold approach that is long term in nature. When you use a long-term investment method, you do not sell the stocks quickly and will hold your position for as long as possible. Penny stock trading on the other hand is more like speed dating. The only way you can meet your profit targets is to sell the stock as soon as possible. It is important never to cling to a penny stock. This can spell disaster for you.

Let us look at an example. A person conducted in of research and what stocks of a very good company in the real estate industry. Two days after he purchased stock, the price of the stock increased by 10%. Over the next three days the price of the stock went up by another 10%. At the end of the first week, the person would have made a profit of 20% had he sold the stock immediately. If you were a good trader, you would sell the stock immediately. You made a profit of 20%, and that is a huge gain.

If you are inexperienced or stubborn, you may want to hold on to that stock under the assumption that the prices will continue to increase. You will make multiple excuses using technical charts or fundamental analysis to convince yourself that you should hold onto that stock. If you are lucky, the price of the stock will not dip. This will convince you to hold onto the stock for longer periods.

During the following weeks, the price of the stock will decrease, and the return on investment will go down. This is still remarkable for a long investment in a penny stock. That said, if you had liquidated the stock earlier when you noticed the rise in prices, you would have made a higher profit. If you continue to hold onto the stock under the impression that it is a correction measure or a bullish trend you are wrong. The price of the stock is not going to follow a bullish trend for eternity. You will suffer losses if you do not liquidate the stock on time. The user who had invested on the stock and held onto it for a long period made huge losses on the position. If the person liquidated the stock earlier, they could have earned higher profit. The person refused to sell fast, and it is for this reason that he or she suffered the consequences. You must remember that greed is your worst enemy when it comes to penny trade stocking.

Do not rely on what the management says

It is true that the testimonies of any product or service provided by a company are important. This information will give you an idea of how good or bad the product or service is. A customer who gives reviews of any product or service is a good source of information. This customer will not be biased towards the company and will not benefit from the sales of the product or service provided by that company. If it is known that a business pays people to review its products or services, traders or investors will refrain from investing in that company. Promotions and testimonials have to be free of bias. This means that there should be no ulterior motive behind the testimony. One should perceive that these testimonies are independent of any influence.

When the management releases any statements, it is important that you take the information with a grain of salt. It is better to disregard this information altogether. You may ask why. The management works hard to improve the view of the company in the public eye. There is a possibility that they are not being truthful about the company since they want to traders to purchase stocks from their company. This will increase the price of the stock in the market. When the stock price increases and the number of buyers increases, the management can raise funds to operate the business. There is very limited information available about companies issuing Penny stocks, which makes it difficult to validate the information or claims made by the management regarding the corporate performance and health of that company.

That being said, the management of any penny stock company is innocent until proven otherwise. It is for this reason that you should only trust the information that they provide if you have enough data to back that information. It is also important that you check online forums to understand what other people feel about the specific penny stock company. These forums will shed some light on how people perceive the trend of the stock to move in the future.

You cannot entirely disregard the statements made by the management about the company. You should rely on this information in conjunction with other information to reduce the risk of making a loss.

Never Sell Short

Short selling is an activity where you sell a stock whose price is dipping. You cannot make a profit when you hold onto this stock. The price of these stocks will continue to decrease which will lead to a loss. You often short sell those stocks that you do not own. You borrow a few stocks from a seller, and sell those stocks once the price decreases. You must ensure that you return the same number of shares you bought to the person or institution you bought the shares from. This is a popular strategy among traders in a market where the price of stocks on a downtrend. This type of market is known as a bear market. The idea behind this strategy is to sell stocks at a higher price today and buy the same security later from the seller at a lower price. This is just a variant of buying low and selling high, but in this strategy, you first sell instead of buying.

Short selling is one of the best strategies to use if you are an experienced trader. This strategy will allow you to make a profit even when the stock price is on a decline. There is, however, a huge risk behind using the strategy to purchase securities, especially when it comes to penny stock trading. Penny stock trading, by itself, is a high risk and volatile trading method when compared to trading in stocks listed in the stock exchange. Short selling penny stocks will increase your risk of making huge losses. Unlike regular stocks, penny stocks are not listed on organized stock exchange boards. Penny stocks are only quoted on the OTC board and as mentioned in the first chapter, there is no law that these stocks should be registered with the stock exchange commission. The companies issuing penny stocks are not required to submit financial statements. It is for this reason that the price of any stock is volatile and can be manipulated. These factors significantly affect the price of the stock. Since the prices can be manipulated, the price of the penny stock can increase if you use this trading strategy leaving you in a position where you make losses.

You may often wonder if it is a good idea to sell a stock short if it is doing badly. You must remember that you only increase the chaos or exacerbate the situation for yourself and your peers when you sell stocks that do badly in the market. Always remember to be patient regardless of what the situation is. Another reason why short selling is a disadvantage for you is that there may be a decrease in the number of stocks available in the future. Most companies only issue a certain volume of Penny stocks when compared to regular stocks. Therefore, when you need to buy enough stocks to make a profit, they may not be enough volume for you to do so. This will lead to huge losses.

Since penny stock trading is risky, it is recommended that you avoid using the trading strategy if you do not have enough experience with trading.

Focus on high trading volumes

You do know that one of the key issues of Penny stock trading is liquidity. The only way you can measure liquidity is by assessing the volume of stocks that is being traded. The larger the volume of stocks being traded, the greater the chances of you making a profit since the price of the stock will increase. When the price of the stock increases, buyers will be interested in purchasing the stock. This will give you a chance to sell the stock and exit the investment quickly. If you trade in a penny stock that has few stocks, that is the volume is low, you will increase your liquidity risk. This means that you cannot liquidate your shares on time and at the price you want to make a profit. You may wonder when it is a good time for you to trade in penny stocks. As a beginner it is important that you only trade in penny stocks if the daily trading volume is at least 100,000 shares. If some stocks have a lower volume, avoid investing in those stocks.

Let us understand this through an example. There are two stocks penny stock A and penny stock B. Let us say that you bought 100,000 shares of Penny stock A at $0.20 per share. This will make the total purchase cost $20, 000. In scenario A, PSA's stock price went up to $0.25 per share for a paper profit of $0.05 per share or

$5,000 equal to a return-on-investment of 25%, which is quite a lot. If PSA's daily average trading volume is just, say, 50,000 shares, you won't be able to unload all your shares at $0.25 per share. You'll have to sell the remaining 50,000 shares the next day but there's a chance the price will have changed by then. Good if it goes up, but if it goes down to, say $0.23 per share, your trading profit for the 50,000 remaining shares will just be $0.03 per share or $1,500 and if you add it to the ones you already sold earlier, your total profit goes down to only $4,000 from $5,000 initially. That's a difference of $1,000 or 20%!

In scenario B, PSA's stock price goes down to $0.19 the day after and you decide to liquidate. If the stock's average daily trading volume is high, proceeds of the sale of all 100,000 shares of PSA will yield you $19,000 or a loss of $1,000 on your $20,000 investment – a 5% loss on investment. If average daily trading volume, however, is at only 50,000 shares, you'll have to share the other half of your holdings the day after. If assuming for the sake of argument that the share price of PSA falls further to $0.18 per share, your proceeds for the remaining half of the shares will only be $9,000. Adding up the proceeds of the 50,000 shares sold at $0.19 per share – total of $9,500 – and the second 50,000 at $0.18 per share, total proceeds will be $18,500, which is $500 less than if you were able to sell the stocks the day before. That translates to an additional 3% loss on your $20,000 investment that brings your loss on investment from only 5% to 8%.

Create and implement trading stops

What is a trading stop? A trading stop is the price level that you determine as an action figure for you to either buy or sell stocks. These stops are termed as take profit triggers or stop loss limits. The latter is the price at which you will liquidate your stocks to minimize or limit your losses. The former is a price at which will liquidate your stocks to realize a profit.

So, why should you setup or create a trading stock? It is important for you to do this to prevent your emotions from clouding your judgment about trading. A classic example of using emotions to trade it is given in the example in the sell fast section in this chapter. Your emotions will change your judgement, which will make it hard to trade and make a profit. Many traders can confirm this since they may have experienced logic when they chose to listen to their heart and not base their decisions on logic.

What should the ideal trading stop limit be for you? The answer to this question will lie in your capacity to take risks. You should ask yourself how much loss you can tolerate in terms of the dollar and percentage value. For example, if you determine that your limit is 5%, your profit levels can be anywhere above 5%.

This trading tactic is easy because it is easy to determine your trading stops. The challenge is to implement the stops, because you need to go up against your emotions. It is important that you never underestimate your emotions. You must be strong and resist the urge to listen to your emotions, and buy or sell a penny stock depending on which limit the price of the stock has hit. Your stops will not predict what will happen to a penny stock price, but they will help you reduce the risk of trading with your heart. This will help you rely on logic that will increase your success in penny stock trading.

Never Settle for Less

When you are out shopping for a house, car, television, coffee maker or even looking for a spouse, you will never settle for anything less than what gives you the best value. So, why should you not do this in Penny stock trading? You must remember that if you choose the wrong penny stock, it can lead to huge losses.

When I say that you need to choose the right penny stock for trading, I am talking about choosing the company that has great earnings. It is also important that you understand how the penny stock prices are doing. You must also look at the average trading volumes of the penny stocks of that company. Let us first understand why you should look at the earnings of the company. The value of any stock, regular or penny, is based greatly on the income of the company. This is especially true about any future income that the company may make. It is important to understand that a company that does not have good earnings currently will not necessarily do well in the future since the company cannot generate a great income. You must, therefore, base your expectations on rationality.

Let us now look at penny stock trading volumes. You do not necessarily have to buy 100,000 shares of stock of a company that has great earnings, especially if the company only has an average daily trade of 5,000 shares. You can only make a profit if you sell the shares that you hold at a price higher than your purchasing price. If you do not sell the shares at the right time, you will not make a profit. Regardless of how high the price of a stock goes, the profit you can make will just be paper profit if you still hold on to that stock. You should remember the concept of liquidity and how important it is that you make a profit when you trade. If the price of a penny stock is high and you have a large volume of that stock, you will potentially make a profit. If a penny stock has reached its highest price, it may not make sense to purchase that stock. Investors believe that the price of stocks that have reached this level will begin to fall. So, avoid investing in these stocks.

Limit your Position Size

It is important to remember that the penny stock profit or losses are only a function of price movements and position size. The position size refers the number of shares that you hold. Therefore, people believe that the larger number of shares that you own the higher the chances of you making a profit or loss depending on the price of that share. It is for this reason that you should consider the number of shares you own against the number of shares of that company in the market. This is the only way you can strike a balance between making a profit or a loss.

Another reason why most experts recommend that you limit the position size is because of liquidity. Your liquidity risk is directly proportional to the position size. This means that if you have higher position size, your liquidity risk automatically increases. If you have a smaller position size, when compared to the average trading volume, it is easier to liquidate the stocks to maximize the profit and minimize the loss.

So how do you determine what your optimal position size is when you trade in Penny stocks? You can do this in two ways. You could either use the risk tolerance approach or the liquidity approach. If you use the liquidity approach, you should limit the number of shares in the position size of a penny stock to a small percentage of the daily trading volume. If the daily trading volume of a specific share is 100,000 shares, you can limit your position size to 20% or 30% of that volume. If you choose to follow the risk tolerance upload to identify the position size, you must determine the maximum loss that you can tolerate in terms of dollar amount and percentage amount. You can use the following formula to determine the number of shares in terms of a percentage:

$ Maximum Position Size = Maximum Loss in $ Amount ÷ Maximum Loss in %

For example, you determined your loss tolerances at 5% and $100 per trade, your position size using the formula would be:

Maximum Position Size = $100 ÷ 5%

Maximum Position Size = $2,000

Once you determine your position size in $ terms, simply calculate the number of shares by dividing the amount over the current trading price to determine your maximum position size in terms of shares.

Forget about Love

It is true that when you love someone too much it will kill you. The same can be said about penny stocks. If you love a penny stock too much or are attached to it, you will never let go of the stock when you are supposed to. This will increase your risk of making a loss while trading in Penny stocks. An investor may be attached to a penny stock for the following reasons: relying only on management statements, following newsletters all emails for focusing only on success stories or reading incorrect information about the stock. So, how do you ensure that you remain detached from your favorite penny stock?

The first thing you need to do is to be content when you achieve or slightly exceed your expected profit. This is a good way to control your biggest weakness, which is greed. Going back to the example in the selling fast section of the chapter, we noted that the trader was greedy and did not want to sell the shares when he should have because he believed that he could make a larger profit by holding onto the stock. He noticed that the price of the stock was increasing every week and chose to sit on the stock under the assumption that it will continue to increase.

Some traders often choose to invest in those penny stocks where people have had the most success. This is called survivorship bias. You can overcome this bias by conducting thorough research on penny stock trading, and understand the different stories around penny stock trading, including the failure stories. When you read these failure stories, you will learn to ground your expectations. This will reduce your attachment to Penny stocks.

Finally, you should reduce your reliance or dependence on the management press releases. The information in these releases will not always be true. As mentioned earlier, it is important that you always take the statement with a grain of salt. You should validate the information in these releases using other sources of information. The management will speak in favor of the company since their bonuses or profit will increase if the stock prices increases. You should validate the statement made by the management using the financial statements that the company releases, reading information on discussion groups or following the news about the penny stocks. You can also follow up any stock expert to understand the trend of a specific penny stock.

Chapter 15

Rules To Swear By

When you want to invest in penny stocks, you must be aware of some important factors. The first thing you should do is to identify ways to cut back on your losses. Never make an investment or trade based on your intuition or your ego. You cannot let emotions drive your decisions. When you know that you made an incorrect investment, you should fix it immediately. Make sure that you track the progress of your investment and watch the stock market closely. Use trend analysis to assess the trend of that stock. If you find that the stock is moving in the same direction that you predicted, relax and wait for the price of the stock to increase. If you, however, see that the price is fluctuating or decreasing in a way that you had not thought, you should sell that stock immediately, even if you only make a little profit from it.

Remember to focus only on the small gains. In the penny stock market, you can only make small gains. If you wait too long to trade, you will lose out on any profit that you may have made had you sold the stock earlier. You will make a big profit if you add all the small profits you make. As mentioned earlier, the penny stock market is the easiest place for an investor to start short since the stocks always follow a pattern. It is easy for both amateurs and experts to predict the trend of the stock. On any day, you can predict that the trend of the stock with a probability of seventy percent, and you should use this information to your advantage.

You can also consider penny stocks to be a long and short hold investment. It is difficult to pick only one strategy and use that while you make an investment. You should use your knowledge about penny stocks to determine which stock can be a long or short investment.

Most purists dislike the penny stocks market since they are averse to the idea of investing in a market that is predictable. They want to take the risk and invest in markets where the prices of the stock fluctuate. If you are an amateur, you should not do this. You can think of the penny stock market as the best place to test your skills. When it comes to penny stocks, you will continue to invest in the stocks until you are satisfied. Remember to record your investments and track the trend of those investments regularly.

As mentioned earlier, it is important that you have a robust Internet connection if you wish to invest in penny stocks. This means that you must invest in a good connection if you want to make the most of this market. Make sure you have a substitute to help you connect to the Internet in case of emergencies.

Never underestimate the value of a stock. If the stock is undervalued, it does not mean that you should not invest in that stock. You may miss out on making big profits when you do this. That being said, if the stock is illiquid, you should avoid investing in it. An illiquid stock is one that looks great on paper but has not been traded in the market. You should determine the level of risk you want to take depending on the market situation. You should look at the market and assess the mood before you make the most of it. If your data says the market is doing great and will continue to do great for some time, you can make large investments. On the other hand, if the market looks drab and dull then it is best that you do not invest in it.

Never believe everything you read about. It is important that you make all your decisions on the data you collect. That said, you should ensure that the data you collect comes from reliable sources. Look at the different sources of data before you determine whether the news about a stock or company in the market is accurate.

There are times when the value of penny stocks deteriorates to a new low, but these stocks will recover well. If you do not want to wait that long, you should make the right calculations and observe the market to see when you need to sell the stock

Chapter 16

Answers to the Top 20 Most Common Questions

You will have some questions about penny stocks when you decide to trade in them. This chapter will cover some of the common questions that people ask about penny stocks.

Are penny stocks a part of the stock market?

Most amateurs have this question, and it is important to understand that penny stocks are a part of the stock market. These are a part of NASDAQ and the New York Stock Exchange. You should speak to your broker to help you find the right stocks to invest in and choose from those stocks. Make sure that you start off with stocks that are prices lower than $5. Some brokers may suggest that you trade in pink sheets, but it is not recommended that you do. Penny stocks are also issued over the counter, and this is the most preferred method.

Are penny stocks good for me?

Penny stocks are a good choice as an investment for both amateurs and established traders. Penny stocks will help you understand how the stock market works. Once you begin trading in penny stocks, you will understand how the price of the stocks rise and fall. You will also learn when to hold or sell the stocks. It is best to look at the market as an outsider before you begin to invest in the market. Once you have the confidence to do so, you can begin to invest in the stock market. Penny stocks will pay you good money if you have enough time to understand the market and know which stock to pick. If you have been investing in the stock market, then you can easily identify the stock market and make a smooth transition. You should identify the difference between penny stock trading and regular stock trading and formulate a strategy to make it big.

Is it for beginners?

Penny stocks are not only for beginners and not for amateurs. Anybody can invest in penny stocks and diversify their portfolio to make good money out of the investments that they make. You do not have to be an expert or well-versed in the stock market to invest in stocks. All you need is some information about the stock market and how it operates. Since you can invest on any number of penny stocks, this is a great choice of investment for beginners.

Can I make good profit from it?

It is easy for you to generate good profit from your penny stock investment. A penny stock works very differently when compared to a regular stock. These stocks are bought when the market opens and sold before the market closes. So, you will know if you have made a profit or loss at the end of the day. Most people make profits on these stocks since they are volatile. They purchase the stocks at a high price and sell them at a higher price within a few minutes. This will give them a chance to make a big profit.

How much should I invest in it?

The amount you want to invest is dependent on how much you want to spare. You should decide on the amount and set it aside. You can invest an amount as low as $50 or as high as $1000. You can maintain a wide investment range when you invest in penny stocks but remember that practice will make you perfect. You can only decide the best rate based on your experience. You will know how much money you should have in your account based on that experience.

Is it easy to trade penny stocks?

It is easy for one to trade in penny stocks. You do not have to be an expert in math or the stock market. All you need is some knowledge about the market and begin trading in the market. This book will help you understand penny stocks and also learn more about trading in penny stocks. You will learn to trade with ease. Most of your doubts about penny stocks will be cleared through this book. The information in this book will allow you to make lucrative decisions about penny stocks.

Is it sustainable?

Penny stocks are sustainable options. The information in this book will help you invest in penny stocks for a long time. If you buy and sell penny stocks on the same day, you will learn to do this for a long time. It can be for one year or more depending on your financial capabilities. It only takes enough faith and patience to learn the trade. If you have both, you can see positive results. It may take you some time to understand how to trade in penny stocks to reap the rewards.

Are there risks involved?

There are numerous risks involved with trading in penny stocks. You must understand these risks and decide your plan of action based on that understanding. When you are aware of what can go wrong, you will be prepared to cater to that risk.

Can I sell them short?

Yes, you can sell the stocks short. It is, however, not advisable that you sell these stocks short. The objective is to make enough money out of your penny stock investments. If you sell these stocks short, then you cannot make that money back. If the penny stock does not fare well and you hold onto that stock for a long time, it is okay to sell that stock short. You can move that money into a better stock.

Can I stop anytime?

Yes, you can stop investing in penny stocks at any time. You can choose when to start or stop trading in penny stocks. If you believe that you have made enough profit and have had your fill, you can stop investing in those stocks. That said, it is important that you decide with all the facts placed in front of you. You can start trading in penny stocks whenever you like.

Can I only invest in penny stocks?

You can choose to invest only in penny stocks. If you want to make money, you can invest in other stocks as well. That being said, if you choose to invest only in penny stocks, you will need to trade carefully since you will invest your entire capital only in one type of stock. It is always a good idea to diversify your risk and not invest only in one type of stock. It is, however, your decision to make since it is your money that you will be investing in the stock. If you adhere to the rules of the trade and are avoid making mistakes, you will not lose money.

Can you become rich?

Yes, the story of Jordan Belfort is true. It is possible for you to make millions of dollars from your penny stock investments. You can only do this when you remain alert and conduct thorough research to understand these investments better. This book will shed some information on both fundamental and technical analysis. You can use these methods to help you assess the value of the stock before you choose to buy or sell that stock. Make sure that you purchase undervalued stocks and sell them at a higher value whenever you can!

Should I sign up somewhere?

There is no company that requires you to sign up before you invest in penny stocks. If you do want to consult an expert and understand the trading better, then you should visit a reliable website and speak to an expert. That said, ensure that you do not sign up to a website that looks suspicious. Make sure that you sign up to a company that will help you identify the right stocks to invest in. Since people view the market differently, it is important that you assess the price in the right way and invest in the right stock to improve your portfolio.

Will I get regular recommendations?

If you sign up to a company, you will get daily recommendations. If you choose to do this on your own, you should stick to a reliable news channel and understand the market based on what the experts are saying. You can also choose stocks based on how you believe they will do in the market. If you have a broker, you can ask them to suggest the right stocks for you since they will receive the right information from the stock market analysts. You should never blindly take everything that they have to offer you. Make sure that you conduct thorough research before you decide. Penny stocks are very predictable, and it is easy to understand the pattern they may follow. Observe the stocks well, and also collect data from the right sources to back your decisions.

Will they give me a stop loss price?

If an analyst or an expert has given a suggestion, they will also include a stop loss suggestion. It is important that you understand the stop loss strategy since it prevents you from choosing bad stocks every time you make a purchase. It is a good idea to get rid of a bad stock and never look at it until there is a change in the way the stock is priced. Some suggest that you ignore the stop loss strategy and continue to hold onto that stock. This will, however, turn into a long-term investment and your money will be locked for a long period. It is always a good idea to sell that stock and make a small loss, which you can compensate for later. You can assign a stop loss price for yourself. This price is the amount of risk you are willing to take. Make sure that you set the stop loss price after you determine the price to which the stock can fall.

What's the best trade strategy?

Remember that trading strategies vary from person to person. You cannot expect to follow a universal strategy. If you want to choose the contrarian strategy, then do that. If you want to use the fundamental strategy, make sure that you have collected the necessary information that will help you invest wisely. If you want to invest in penny stocks using technical knowledge, you can do that too. You can choose the trade strategy that will work best for you. Do not trust another person's strategy since what has worked for them does not necessarily have to work for you. You may start off with the same capital as your friend, but this does not mean that both of you will make wise decisions. The profit or loss you make is dependent on your trading skills. So, ensure that you choose the right trading strategy for you.

Is there a minimum capital required?

There is no minimum capital that you should invest in when it comes to the stock market. Since there is a lot of risk associated with the stock, it is important to choose the right stocks to invest in. It is always a good thing to start off with a small capital, and then increase the capital as you go along. It is only when you do this that you will know what you are getting yourself into and whether or not you want to add more capital. Some socks will require you to invest a minimum amount, but since the price of those stocks is low you do not have to spend too much money to invest in those stocks. If you have enough money to invest, you can diversify your risks and investments. You should always try to invest only 5% of the money in a stock. If you invest more then you will lose more than what you can afford. You will constantly worry about your money. Make sure that you have a sizeable amount of money that you can invest in different stocks.

Does it need full time attention?

No, it is not important for you to continuously monitor penny stocks. Numerous professionals invest in penny stocks. You do not have to constantly stare at the screen and observe the fluctuations. All you need to do is set alerts that will tell you whether a stock is moving in the right direction. Make sure that you also know how to take quick action. You can also ask your broker to assist you. This person will observe the stocks and look at the trend. They will also tell you when it is the right time to either buy or sell these stocks. If you are serious about investing in penny stocks, it is important that you spend some time to understand these stocks better. It is only when you do this that you can trade regularly in the market. If you want to quit your job and become a full-time trader, you can do that too. It is a risky thing to do to take up penny stock trading full-time since there are numerous risks associated with it.

Can I trade daily?

The penny stock trading is a form of day trading. People are meant to buy the stocks and sell them on a daily basis to make small profits. So, you should choose the right stocks. Make sure that the stocks are volatile and the price either goes up or down. Be careful and choose those stocks whose prices you can predict. Choose the stocks whose prices drop during the first few hours of the day and rise at the end of the day. That way, you can buy at a lower value and sell at a higher value.

Can I hold and earn?

You can earn even if you choose to hold onto penny stocks. The price of some penny stocks will increase overnight, so you should take advantage of that situation. You should, however, know when to hold onto a stock and when to sell it. Some stocks will lose points overnight, so it is important that you sell that stock on the same day before the market closes. Do not get carried away because you will make some mistakes. If you continue to hold onto a bad stock, you will not make a profit. That being said, if you choose to hold onto that stock for a long period, you can make a profit in the future. There may be a time when you invest in penny stocks from the same industry, which will make you lose some money. So, make the right decisions and choose wisely.

I hope this chapter answered some or all of your questions about penny stocks

Conclusion

If you are looking to make money quickly and efficiently, then you must invest in penny stocks. There are only a handful of people who are adept at investing in penny stocks. Over the course of this book you will have gathered information on what penny stocks are, and the best ways to trade in penny stocks. If you want to invest in penny stocks, you only need to follow the different techniques in this book so you can make money.

If you are an amateur, you are bound to make some mistakes in the beginning. It is okay to make these mistakes as long as you learn from them. Experienced traders too learned from their own mistakes. It is their experience that helps them act in the right way to make a profit regardless of the condition of the market.

I hope the information in this book helps you excel at trading in penny stocks.

References

https://www.udemy.com

https://economictimes.indiatimes.com/definition/Penny-Stock

https://economictimes.indiatimes.com/marketstats/pid-414,sortorder-desc,sortby-weekPercentChange.cms

https://investorplace.com/2015/05/penny-stocks-investing-myths/

https://www.benzinga.com/general/education/19/01/12938249/3-myths-about-penny-stocks

https://www.dummies.com/personal-finance/investing/penny-stocks/penny-stock-misconceptions/

https://www.wallstreetdaily.com/2018/05/04/penny-stock-frequently-asked-questions/

https://www.timothysykes.com/blog/answering-20-penny-stock-trading-faqs/

https://www.marketwatch.com/story/10-ways-to-trade-penny-stocks-2012-02-03

https://www.investopedia.com/articles/investing/092214/how-pick-winning-penny-stocks.asp

https://www.investopedia.com/penny-stock-trading-4689659

https://bullishbears.com/penny-stock-trading-strategies/

https://www.adigitalblogger.com/research/fundamental-analysis-of-stocks/

https://www.investopedia.com/terms/f/fundamentalanalysis.asp

https://www.udemy.com/course/trade-wSith-technical-analysis

Made in the USA
Monee, IL
22 March 2020